exObjects

the art of holding on, letting go

exObjects

the art of holding on, letting go

Edited by

A.T. Boyle and Shinie Antony

Om Books International

First published in 2024 by

Om Books International

Corporate & Editorial Office
A-12, Sector 64, Noida 201 301
Uttar Pradesh, India
Phone: +91 120 477 4100
Email: editorial@ombooks.com
Website: www.ombooksinternational.com

Sales Office
107, Ansari Road, Darya Ganj
New Delhi 110 002, India
Phone: +91 11 4000 9000
Email: sales@ombooks.com
Website: www.ombooks.com

ISBN: 978-81-19750-56-6

Printed in India

10 9 8 7 6 5 4 3 2 1

for Mum and Dad,
Corin and Calla
– A.T. Boyle

for the little boy my father once was
– Shinie Antony

Contents

Introduction

A.T. Boyle

Beginnings beguile.

Many of us dedicate time in the present to grasping the past. In childhood our scope is the particular, but even then, curiosity fills gaps and extends awareness beyond the physical limits of an early dependent world. As our responsibilities and distractions expand, some things are forgotten. And too often it's only when a continuum is interrupted that we stop and notice, make time, return our attention to the particular.

Every piece in this book scrutinises motivations, actions and perspectives over time, a process that locates unique graces through sympathetic and frequently humorous portraits.

Each beginning was an object, something that might or might not be tangible but has a continuing presence. It is when interrogating the minutest characteristic that opportunities appear for others to perceive the microcosm of a rendered world. It is exactly here that we might attach our own emotions and expand understanding.

Acts of creative expression require risk-taking. The writers in this anthology took risks, whether by being more open about grief or love or hope, or more honest about shortcomings and achievements. The collection, balancing human and natural environments, comprises the way writers have tussled with concepts that may otherwise seem unfathomable. Perhaps an event happened long ago, or information was hidden or otherwise lost.

The stories have much in common.

Teak used in the making of a rural doorframe in Devasiachan Benny's account becomes associated with a piece of furniture made in the same hardwood, this time fabricked for a chair beloved by Shinie Antony's dad. Both stories encompass crafted wood and growth and community and personal history. They resolve into contemporary rationales about heritage saved, sometimes only by writing about it.

A flotsam dressing table that has surfaced through generations of Shashi Deshpande's family connects to wooden chemistry benches in my own.

Gajra Kottary's interest lies in the way silk cloth expresses her father's personality, while experiences of cotton cloth came via my grandmothers who wove yards and yards for others to make sheets and garments. Jaishree Misra writes of elegant women wearing coats over saris and the strong sway of a childhood home; Ramona Sen provides perspectives on ties; and the cloth of childhood engendered by Jerry Pinto attaches to the reminiscences of Sauma Afreen and Devasiachan Benny – the youngest writers in this collection, who look back less far but no less compellingly at the impact of human behaviour on our planet. While Belinda RushJansen reveals what immersion in nature feels like, through a brass candlestick lit through the years.

Alongside the particularities of a scene and the players within it you will find tragedy, fastidiousness, wit, plenty of pride. Vikram Sampath convinces us of the power of good food and conversation to promote empathy, and musicality appears often, not least serving to unite Shinie Antony's dad and mine in the present.

Running through the collection is compassion. All of our chosen objects serve as a nexus of the emotional interactions that bind us to people and place. Some objects accumulate importance over the years, but an object discovered will not always result in a wish to keep it, and these stories throw up challenges that will hopefully push readers towards puzzlements of their own.

Before ending this beginning, though, I must mention my co-editor Shinie. In pinging ideas and phrases back and forth between England and India she brought much joy and generosity and clarity, as well as her practical drive to get on.

Introduction

Shinie Antony

Our house is littered with his stuff. Watch, umbrella, belt, glasses, shoes, naval medals… A birthday card he gave my mom is open at *To My Darling Lily*.

It was with great care that I transported my father's favourite easy chair from his house in Kochi to Bengaluru, where I live. I toyed briefly with changing the blue striped canvas, but then decided to retain it, ostensibly because it added to the antique look, but also because I was loathe to interfere with a memory – of him reclining on it first thing in the morning to read the newspaper on his sunny porch.

He inherited the easy chair from his father, who died young. He also brought a clock from his ancestral home in Thrissur, Kerala. A large wooden clock with Roman numerals and a pendulum that rang the whole house like a bell.

When Alison (A.T. Boyle) first told me about exObjects, her understanding of loss and grief as well as commitment to micro-histories compelled me to look at my own surroundings and the objects in them more closely. The obits she wrote – she lost both her parents during the Covid years – held up unexpected objects, and via them the importance and comfort we attach to them. These objects, pixelating dully in the background until then as mundane possessions of others, suddenly start to glisten. In time grief loses its raw flamboyance and settles down into a prosaic number of finite things left behind, those articles of continuum and belonging, carrying within them words and voices, quirks and little eccentricities. Entire people, actually.

The clock, like the easy chair, is a portable object of continuity. They don't just belong to him or to us; they are daily everyday snapshots of where we come from, who we used to be. The present is the past.

1

REFLECTIONS

Shashi Deshpande

Novelist and short-story writer **Shashi Deshpande** is the author of ten novels, two novellas, nine short-story collections and four books for children. Her novel *That Long Silence* has received the Sahitya Akademi award. *The Dark Holds No Terrors*, *A Matter of Time* and *Small Remedies* are her other noted novels. Her latest novel is *Strangers to Ourselves*. She also has three books of non-fiction, *Listen to Me*, *Writing from the Margin* and *Subversions*.

Her short stories and novels have been translated into a number of Indian as well as European languages. She herself has translated some works from Kannada and Marathi into English. She was awarded the Padma Shri in 2008, and in 2023 she was given the Lifetime Achievement Award by the Times of India group.

'After having been very reticent about myself all my life, I wrote my memoirs in which I had to discard the reticence. Since then, it seems to have become easier and easier to write about personal matters. This essay is one of those. No more, I tell myself. Time to stop before I begin wallowing in personal revelations. But it was such a pleasure to invoke my parents, my grandfather and his girl-wife. Lost somewhere in the recesses of my mind, they boldly presented themselves when I needed them. It was a pleasure meeting them.'

A Hindu marriage is considered a sacrament. Ironically, however, an arranged Hindu marriage is often preceded by most business-like negotiations, the marriage being regarded as finalised only when the two parties, the bride's family and the groom's, reach a satisfactory agreement. In all matters the groom's family has the upper hand; the bride's family has but to concur with their wishes. This is how it was and, in many cases, still how it is.

By the standards of arranged marriages of the time, my parents' wedding, which took place nearly ninety years back, has to be looked at as an oddity. In spite of having heard the story of their marriage and of having read about it in the book my mother wrote on her life with her husband, for me, the mystery still remains: why did her family, a very well-to-do family, get her married to a man who had nothing but the salary he earned as a lecturer in a government college? Equally damning should have been the fact that he didn't seem to have a family; he came for the wedding with just a few friends. That he had cut himself off from his family because he could not live as they did, a life strictly contained within the rigid rules of caste, would not explain or condone his behaviour; in fact, it would be considered a greater fault. Even more strange was the fact that the groom did not ask for a dowry – this, when he could have made extravagant demands because the bride's family was a fairly wealthy one. Landowners, my grandfather and his three brothers were also successful professionals.

This is not all. Even more curious is the question of language. My mother from Pune, knowing only Marathi, and my father, a Kannada man who knew a smattering of Marathi because he had studied in a Pune college, though he was never comfortable with it – how did her family imagine they would communicate? In effect, why did the bride's family decide to marry her off to a man who was no match for their daughter? Was it because of his England-returned tag? After all, it did mean something in those days. As for the couple, they were clear: the man chose the girl because she was educated. She was a graduate in the days when few girls went to college, perhaps even to school. And the bride was happy with her family's choice because she was fascinated by the fact that he was a writer. Besides, as she often confessed later, she was also attracted by his unusualness.

How unusual he was she came to know the moment she entered her new home. It was bare, without a stick of furniture! My father's landlord had given him a table and a chair in the hope that the man would marry his sister. When, instead, he returned from Pune with a bride, the landlord, in a fit of pique, promptly took away the table and chair. My father was writing his first novel then. It was a daily deadline project, with the publisher, a novice like his author and in a hurry to establish himself as a publisher, coming every evening to take away the pages written that day. My father, therefore, could not stop writing. So, he continued to write, sitting on the floor, and using a steel trunk as a table. I imagine the publisher did get his daily quota of material.

News of his daughter's furniture-less situation must have reached my grandfather, Babasaheb Chandrachud. And there soon came to my parents some pieces of furniture from the prestigious Army and Navy Stores in Bombay. A prosperous lawyer, my grandfather unstintingly bought the best. A very generous-sized bed of mahogany, with bedposts that went up in elegant swirls to a shining mahogany grape-shaped top. A writing table, covered with green baize, almost half the size of a billiards table perhaps, with two chairs that fitted snugly into the kneehole. There was also a dressing table with a beautiful oval mirror and drawers that moved in and out silently and smoothly.

The landlord, if he had seen this stuff, especially the writing table, would have gnashed his teeth in rage. However, by then my father had risen in the hierarchy of teachers in the college and was given a large sprawling bungalow as his residence. Built for British officials, it had a formal garden, surrounded by a wilderness of bushes and rooms for servants to live in. The furniture fitted into the large rooms of the bungalow as if custom-made for the house. We grew up here, in this bungalow, among this furniture. India had at the time just crossed the cruel hump of partition and become independent. The country walked carefully between the trauma of partition and the euphoria of independence. Everything was in a fluid state. The long shadow of a receding British rule still lingered. After all, the influence of a century (two, if one included the East India Company period) of domination could not vanish overnight. The bungalow we lived in, our much-admired furniture, even my father's clothes ... all these carried traces of British influence. Yet my father, who had come back from England admiring the British for their liberalism and appreciating the sturdy independence of the working class, was also a great admirer of Gandhi-ji. I remember the day of Gandhi-ji's funeral, the large hall in our house packed with shocked students listening in pin-drop silence to Melville de Mellow on the radio, who broke down even as he was describing the scene of the funeral. And I vividly remember my father in his easy chair, a towel thrown over his face to hide his tears.

Our lives too changed after this. My father resigned from his job, on a 'matter of principle' we were told. We had to move out of our beautiful bungalow and live in a doll-house-sized house. None of our grandfather's gifts could fit into that house; they were sent away we don't know where. In two or three years my father built a house for us (even while he was jobless), a house with rooms large enough to contain my grandfather's gifts, which came back to us. But this was not to last either. My father got a job in Delhi and my parents rented out the house with all it contained to a friend and moved with my brother to Delhi, while my sister and I were to stay in hostels in Bombay. I imagine that the excitement of living in Bombay, as well as the devouring homesickness we suffered – at least I did – made it possible for us to not look back or regret leaving our home behind. After this, for my parents it was a peripatetic life of rented houses and rented furniture. I joined them in Bangalore for a few years. Our old life was forgotten.

After marriage, with children and the beginning of my writing career, I was caught up in the busyness of my life and had no time to think of the early days. Of old possessions. Until a childhood friend came to visit me. During our conversation, she told me that her family had bought our hatstand when my father sold the house. At first I was confused. Hatstand? Did we have a hatstand? Immediately a picture of it flashed before my eyes. Yes, of course, it had been right there, opposite the front door. One of those period pieces with hooks to hang headgear on and a stand for umbrellas. And then it hit me – if my father had sold the hatstand, he must have sold my grandfather's gifts as well. I had not thought of them for a long time, or had perhaps imagined them to be somewhere, waiting for us to reclaim them. But no, they were gone. They were no longer ours. A sharp pang of regret pierced me at the idea of the loss. Had my father sold them casually? Or had he suffered a moment's grief at the loss of what had symbolised his early life, his hopes for his career and the beginning of his family life? But what could he have done with the bed and the table, anyway? There was no room for them in the house my parents ultimately bought and in which they finally settled down. Both of them lived there till the end.

Selling a home your parents had lived in for years, disposing of all that had made up their life for decades, is a melancholy task. And a difficult one. My sister and I put our feelings aside and went through the exercise mechanically. Except for some books I took and my father's manuscripts and awards, neither of us wanted anything. What, then, were we to do with the rest of the stuff? There was such a lot of it. So I thought then. But about twenty-five years later, when I had to do this again, selling our house and moving for safety and convenience to an apartment, I was aghast at the amount of stuff my husband and I had accumulated. Things I never knew we owned tumbled out of cupboards and fell from attics. When had I bought all these things and what had I wanted them for? My parents' collection had been infinitely more modest. I thought then of a character called a Clutter Counselor in Anne Tyler's wonderful novel, *Saint Maybe*. This is someone who helps you to get rid of things periodically. A job most people find hard, since they are hindered both by inertia and a reluctance to part with anything. 'Do you think you will need these in the next month or so? Or in a week? No? Then out it goes.' That's how the Clutter Counselor worked. Ruthlessness – that's what's needed with objects. A ruthlessness I never had. Which few people have.

My parents would certainly never have needed a Clutter Counselor. They bought only what they needed, there was no accumulated clutter. 'Simple living and high thinking' – one of the aphorisms my mother often quoted. It was a habit of hers, making it seem that she believed in and acted according to the maxim she was quoting. Simple living, however, was certainly a part of their lives. It was an austere life they lived. Their needs were minimal. Even clothes, on which we splurge, buying them for more reasons than need, occupied just two shelves in their steel almirah. My mother had given away all her silk saris; only a few cotton saris were left. And my father, who had given up his 'western' clothes many years back, had only a few dhotis, kurtas and one Nehru jacket for occasions. He had lost all his 'English' clothes when a burglar, unable perhaps to find anything valuable in the house, had taken away the trunkful of clothes that looked expensive. I don't think my father regretted the loss of those clothes. After the trauma of his jobless days, he was perhaps relieved to be free of that dapper young England-returned man, who had been so popular with his students and had made his girl students' hearts flutter. (One of his students told me this, the old woman laughing at the memory of her younger romantic self.) In a way, my father remade himself after years of humiliation; he even changed his name. And I thought, if he could give up so many things, especially his name, so much a part of oneself, he was obviously even less attached to objects. Perhaps selling my grandfather's gifts had been no sacrifice.

Yet the truth is that the objects we own are not mere *objects*. They are imbued with our experiences, our emotions, our memories. Memory brings back to me an old brown sweater that my father wore in his old age. He had lost much weight in his last years and the sweater hung on his emaciated frame. 'The shrinkage of old age' as Virginia Woolf called it. But she was speaking of the mind, not of the body. And my father's mind had certainly not shrunk. During a TV interview, responding to a statement of the interviewer, he said, 'I am an intelligent, thinking man.' The words said positively, yet not boastfully. This is me, he was saying. He looked strong and confident as he said the words, no longer a frail old man in a sweater too large for him.

All religions preach against the accumulation of wealth and possessions. The Buddha speaks of desire as the source of grief. The Upanishads say the same thing through stories and conversations. Maitreyi refuses the wealth offered by her philosopher husband Yajnavalkya, and Nachiketas, only a boy but a wise one, rejects Yama's offer of all that he, Nachiketas, desired. Both Maitreyi and Nachiketas opt for knowledge. And there are Jesus Christ's dramatic words that a rich man can no more go to heaven than a camel go through a needle's eye. All of it futile advice. We are human. And therefore slaves to our desires. The ruthlessness the Clutter Counselor advocates is way beyond us. How can you despise objects when the spirit of the age is to acquire? When we are constantly assailed by voices telling us to buy, when we have beautiful people and happy families telling us that they are happy and beautiful because they use this, that or another product? When desires, not really our own, are instilled into us by those who want to sell us their merchandise?

Nevertheless, to be fair to ourselves, it is also true that we are often attached to objects beyond their utility, beyond their monetary value. Objects evoke memories, they are associated with a place or a time. The pang of regret that shot through me when I heard that my father had sold my grandfather's gifts was not because of the objects themselves, or their possible English provenance. Yes, my grandfather's gifts were elegant, they were unique. But that was not why I regretted that they had been sold. Nor was the regret sentimental, because they came from my grandfather. I had scarcely known him; I had been perhaps four when he died. No, my feeling for the objects was mainly because they were associated with the magical days of my childhood. A time when there were siblings to share and quarrel with, friends to play with, a sprawling house and a compound so large, with so many nooks and corners to hide in, that a game of hide-and-seek could go on for hours. There were caring parents in the background, and a father who was a rock on which we could build our future lives. My grandfather's gifts encompassed all these things.

Only the dressing table survived all the changes and moves of my parents' lives. And it is this dressing table, the least treasured of my grandfather's gifts, which carries within it a story that I, as a storyteller, find fascinating. I learnt when I began writing that the past often creeps into the present, that it is difficult to disentangle the two. To think of the dressing table is to remember the kumkum box that my mother brought from her natal home to her marital one. Called a kumkum peti, this box was an object that most married women, of a certain class of course, owned. A wooden box, with a hinged top, the front half of which could be propped up to give women a mirror. A very small mirror, in which a woman could see only portions of her face. In any case, a woman required the mirror only for applying the round dot of kumkum in the middle of her forehead, this being the most important thing in her life; it denoted that her husband was alive. In the peti there was room for a kumkum container (a dry powder then), and one for wax, which provided the foundation for the kumkum, and there was space for a comb and some U-shaped hairpins, to keep the hair knot in order. It was not possible for a woman to have casual, fleeting glimpses of herself in this mirror. Once she had applied her kumkum after her bath, made a straight middle parting in her hair and tied it up, the box had to be put away. No room there for vanity, not even for the most innocent vanity which gives a woman pleasure in seeing her own reflection.

The kumkum box my mother brought to her marital home had been her mother's. My grandmother died of TB. It seems strange to call her a grandmother; she must have died when she was about twenty. My mother once told us that she was not allowed in the room in which her mother was dying, obviously because of the terrible propensity of the disease to infect others. I can imagine the anguish of the woman who could not see her daughter before dying, who knew she was leaving her little daughter motherless. And then, years later, when that daughter got married, her father – my grandfather – sent her a dressing table. Surely it was for her alone? Why would anyone send a male a dressing table? Was he making a statement? Today, when I think of the dressing table, I think with pleasure of a man who sent his daughter the gift of a large mirror, so different from the cramped mirror of the kumkum box. I also think of the cosmetics available today, of the beauty parlours scattered all over cities and towns, to which even schoolgirls and working girls with just a little money go to have their eyebrows tweezed and shaped, to have a manicure and pedicure.

I think of the silence in these places, in which the only sounds are the hum and buzz of machines in which young men and women work on women's hair, their faces, hands, feet and much else. All of them, staff and clients, worshipping the goddess of female beauty.

I often saw my mother looking at herself in the mirror, not admiringly but questioningly. Was she remembering her mother then, a woman whose life ended before it really began? Or her father who later became a champion of women's education, thinking perhaps of his young dead wife? Or was she asking some questions of herself? I don't know. All I know is that my sister and I saw ourselves in the mirror as girls, free birds, and then as young women, later as wives and mothers, struggling to do justice to both the home and career. We managed, though it was hard.

My mother's dressing table is now in my son's house and my daughter-in-law, a courageous and independent woman, is the one the mirror reflects. The mirror has reflected three generations of women, it has been mute witness to their lives. And I, the storyteller, think at times that I can see in the mirror shadowy glimpses of the two men who stood by their women – my grandfather and my father. This, I think with pleasure, is a story with a happy ending.

2

It's Intangible

Devasiachan Benny

One of eight recipients of a Creative Economy Scholarship from the British Council, **Devasiachan Benny** received a Gold award for his extracurricular activities and graduated in Tourism and Cultural Policy from Goldsmiths, University of London, in 2023. He was a Goldsmiths Student Ambassador there. Devasiachan was the youngest person to be invited to attend India Global Forum's Cultural Economy and Creative Industries Summit, co-hosted by the British Council at Nehru Centre, London.

His studies have focused on entrepreneurship in emerging economies and nature-based solutions for climate resilience (HarvardX and edX). He continued his learning along with professional engagements and completed a BA in Vocational History with Archaeology and Museology from St Thomas College in Pala, and an MA in History from Indira Gandhi National Open University. He currently works in London for Thames Clippers.

'An interest in history and tourism drew me to adopt a dual approach to my learning and cultural practice, combining studies in archaeology, museology and history with professional engagements in the south of India and south of England. With a deep sense of loss at my childhood home being disassembled beam by beam, I was fortunate to be able to keep two iron keys (one to open a wardrobe and the other the front door) as well as a few agricultural implements including two teak ploughs. The farming objects are stored in the history museum at Saint Thomas College in Palai for all to see, testifying to the value of rural living: https://www.stcp.ac.in/History_Museum.php. The keys, I have kept. I follow a disciplined life of self-penance. I have eaten a single meal a day for eight years and counting. Taking part in exObjects has encouraged me to interrogate the tangible and intangible elements of what I find to be important, helping to heal my pain. Handheld by many, I continue to be ignited by the values of my grandmother, Grandma Rosamma, who died in 2023. I find happiness in small things. Learning how to read the past and analyse the present gives me a clear sense of direction.'

When I try to sleep inside my newly-built concrete home I hear cars racing, bikes cruising and lorries speeding. I lie confused in my bed. The house is set apart from any highway, so I wonder what I am listening to. Is it my future?

Although this concrete home replaced the teak version of my childhood, its setting remains the lush and hilly landscape of the Western Ghats. And, although many organic smallholdings and biodiverse plantations are gone, along with the jackfruit that interspersed the mighty hardwood trees, I'm still surrounded by greenery and the rhythm of cicadas.

Squadrons of ants still march through my garden, squirrels still leap from guava to jackfruit to custard apple to mulberry to papaya, but the nature around does take a different form. Its system is orderly, matching the requirements of intensive rubber production that replaced paddy field patterns and industry. My father nurtures rubber saplings now, but thankfully he has continued some of the features of that old life. Beehives produce thick combs next to our concrete house, and nuts and fruit ripen for mealtimes.

The revolution at home began when elephants came to manoeuvre the tonnage of felled wood, bettering the mechanical cranes unable to access the steep slopes of the dense plantation. One physical legacy of that wood was a cowshed with capacity for ten animals and agricultural implements for oxen to plough the land. Cut teak made a firewood storehouse longer than a badminton court. It was used for a giant wooden box too, a hide-and-seek playground and a place to sleep in warmth. For adults, that box stored the rice and nutmeg and pepper and ginger and coffee beans and cocoa beans we had harvested. It also had plenty of secret wooden drawers, but the money chest was always empty when I checked.

It's common to find termites in a wooden house, and these insects were loved by the hen. Even the hen's eggs tasted delicious. The door of our dining room was made with four pieces of teak of unquestionable strength. The food cooked on a wood fire in an earthy clay pot tasted unique, tickling my taste buds with spice-infused aroma. The narrow stream swam with me and the fishes, its banks speckled with sugar-crystal sand.

When I was young, I always craved the tender coconut from a nearby tree, which was shared in chunks amongst siblings. The tanginess of passionfruit never persuaded me, but that didn't matter because its abundance was loved by our neighbours, the bats and the birds. Chirruping birds and squirrels feasted on the red-ripe papaya, matching my happiness when a plucked pomelo refreshed me as much as I could wish. Village life certainly had its divinity and purity.

Wooden roofing in the kitchen had been replaced by asbestos sheets because the original caught fire from the rubber-smoking chimney on the floor above. The tiled worktops were faded by ash from the wood-fired chimney that dried our ginger and clove and turmeric. The rest of that childhood house evaded conflagration until it fell to the concrete modern dream.

Weathered teak is often purchased by tourist development organisations for a very low price, then bit by bit the house is reassembled in a resort, fetching a fortune for the corporates. The wooden pieces of my home reside in a place where people are unaware of its family story. Whereas my teak house was naturally temperature-controlled, expensive air conditioning cannot moderate the temperature of its concrete replacement. No matter how cool the dial setting, modernisation cannot take away my feelings of burning and pain. That traditional house hosted three generations and me, the upcoming fourth generation. If I had the wood pieces still, it would be easy to refit them in a new location and accommodate more.

And now, even my concrete home is under threat. Once built, two road alignments called the Greenfield Highway will precisely pass through the house and its surrounding rubber plantation. Compensation will be insufficient to build a hut.

Many agrarian communities live within the highway perimeters. These are sincere people who work hard on farms or in small businesses. Plenty of them have not seen metro-cities or fast-food luxuries. Their life is agriculture, and they are the first and the worst affected by climate change. And, change.

As I see the black polished roads, I rationalise that well-paved and well-connected national networks are essential for ease of transport and trade. I can assure you that travelling via a six-lane highway will mesmerise you. Most definitely this route will boost responsible tourism, and travellers will be surprised by the region's biodiversity gems. I am equally excited to travel by this route to Kovalam, the beach I love the most. The infinite view of ocean there makes me think far and wide, sometimes about England. When I am working in inner city London, I gravitate towards its sky gardens planted with tropical species that thrive in Kerala, looping me back.

I accept that cars and bikes and lorries will roll over some of my hopes. The land survey has begun and in time the government will flatten what is there to speed up movement to and from and past my family home. In the days before a second home is gone, my ears will listen out for the soothing sound of cicadas, and I will yearn to inhale clean air.

Memories of old teak will continue to quilt my dreams, because I own a key.

This key is large, made of iron and rusty. It used to open the front door of the home whose keyhole can no longer be found. When I hold this key, the bussing bees and I begin to circle the passionfruit that wafts its ripened scents to my nostrils, and our narrow stream full of glittering orange-striped fishes begins to ripple.

I stand in the open door of a wooden kitchen sipping water from a clay pot. I watch as a fox sneaks into the garden. I testify to the importance of intangible and tangible heritage.

I was too young for my voice to be heard then. I am speaking now.

3

Ma's Room

Vikram Sampath

Bangalore-based historian **Dr Vikram Sampath** is the author of ten books, including *Splendours of Royal Mysore: The Untold Story of the Wodeyars, Voice of the Veena: S. Balachander, Women of the Records* and *Indian Classical Music and the Gramophone*. His two-volume biography *Savarkar: Echoes from a Forgotten Past* and *Savarkar: A Contested Legacy*, and his latest books, *Bravehearts of Bharat: Vignettes from Indian History, Waiting for Shiva: Unearthing the Truth of Kashi's Gyan Vapi* and *Tipu Sultan: The Saga of Mysore's Interregnum* became national bestsellers. In 2021 Vikram was elected a fellow of the Royal Historical Society. He was awarded the Sahitya Akademi's first Yuva Puraskar in English literature and the ARSC International Award for excellence in historical research in New York for his book *My Name Is Gauhar Jaan: The Life and Times of a Musician*. This book has been adapted for a play, *Gauhar*, by Lillete Dubey. He was among four writers and artists selected as writers-in-residence at the Rashtrapati Bhavan in 2015. Vikram has a doctorate in history and music from the University of Queensland, Australia, and was a senior research fellow at the Nehru Memorial Museum and Library, New Delhi. He was also a fellow of the Aspen

Global Leadership Network, Eisenhower Global Fellow and a visiting fellow at the Wissenschaftskolleg Berlin. Currently, he is an adjunct senior fellow at Monash University, Australia. He is the founder of the Archive of Indian Music and the Foundation for Indian Historical and Cultural Research that fosters new scholarship in Indian history, and curates ARTH: A Culture Fest.

'To look your demons in the eye and bare your heart for the world to read is not a particularly comfortable experience. I didn't expect it to be; hence, I kept postponing it – like an errant schoolboy who shies away from difficult homework. A special someone goaded me to finally write this out. "Remember your ma as part of the healing process, and the nice, sweet things about her will be therapy. Your words will celebrate her life, not mourn her loss." Thanks to those loving words I managed to gather sufficient courage. Sometimes with tears streaming uncontrollably down my face, or prompted to smile or grin widely at other times, I realise that I have lightened a big burden.'

Time seems to have frozen in the little room that she called hers. Since the morning of 18 January 2018, everything in this room – the bedspread, the pillows, the white shawl, the yellow Tupperware bottle of water and the stainless-steel box full of daily medicines – have remained just as they were on that fateful morning. The morning that changed my life irrevocably.

Just two days prior we had celebrated Ma turning sixty-eight. But little did any of us know then that the joys, mirth and laughter would be so short-lived and ephemeral. On that morning, sitting beside my father in our car, headed for her health check-up, even as she was chatting and arguing with him as always, she gently put her head on his shoulder, as though to take a break from the prattle. In a matter of few seconds and perhaps completely unbeknownst to her too, Ma's soul decided to leave, in a quiet, peaceful and blessed manner. As much as I was happy for her great fortune of securing such a peaceful end, the fact that someone who mattered the world to me, was at the epicentre of my existence, had abandoned me in this terribly abrupt manner without a sense of 'closure' (whatever that means), shattered me to smithereens. I had just seen her off from home an hour before, and to so quickly encounter a cold, lifeless 'body', as they call it, that did not exult on seeing me or rise to embrace as she always did, broke something permanently even as it reinforced the uncertainty on which all our lives hinge.

And what does someone who has lost a valuable treasure do? Hold on tightly to the few fragments that remain. Ma's room was thus embalmed since then, possibly to trick myself into believing that things were still the same, and she was very much there as always. Many, many nights have been spent sitting by that bedside where her visage now rests in a photograph with a wide, beatific, radiant smile; sharing my joys and successes, diurnal mundanities, fears and insecurities and, of course, copious tears. In the early months after her departure, quite surreally, from nowhere a strand or two of hair, or her fragrance or the smell of the medicines and oils that she massaged her aching feet with would gently waft through, almost reassuringly, that I am right here and I am very much listening to you gibber.

As the years rolled on, I came to realise that Ma's aura was not and definitely could not be contained within the four walls of that little room. It permeated beyond, through the people she met and interacted with, and ended up leaving an indelible mark on them all. Coming from a lower middle-class Maharashtrian Brahmin family that had been settled in Bangalore for generations, Ma, as the eldest daughter, had responsibilities thrust on her very early in life. With her father paralysed and two younger sisters, the burden of being the breadwinner for the family fell on her. She was of course fortunate to have found a loving partner in my father, whom she met while working in a bank. He unquestioningly agreed to her marriage condition to support their family after marriage – a rarity for men in this country. But the pressures of a chaotic personal and professional life saddled with many responsibilities took their toll and ruined her health irretrievably. From a completely unexpected episode of malignant lung cancer that struck her when she was barely forty-nine, Ma's health went down a rapid slippery slope.

Illness can, of course, hit anyone at any time, any age. But what distinguished Ma was her ability to make light of every pain and suffering and perennially search for silver linings in the darkest of clouds. Her capability to poke fun at herself and dire situations gave us – my father and me – the strength to go through the process of caregiving and helplessly watch her writhe in pain. Not once do I recall self-pity or that famous dramatic questioning to God and the universe, 'Why me?' The clinical acceptance of every proverbial lemon that life threw at her demonstrated a businesslike prowess in making lemonade, an enviable skill revealing resolute inner strength. This positive frame of mind was reflected in the glow and cheerfulness she always exuded. The chatterati she met at my book events would rave about her ethereal beauty, using cheesy lines such as: 'You look too young to be Vikram's mother, more like his elder sister.' And, 'Tell us your beauty routine and the secret of this youthfulness!' In response to most of these annoying queries Ma would chuckle with embarrassment and change the topic. Not one of them realised that her beaming smiles and infectious grace concealed so much physical suffering and pain. However, having doggedly insisted on attending one of my important book launches, flying all the way to Delhi a fortnight after a grievous heart attack (much against the wishes of her cardiologist and my father), she decided to give it back to someone who asked her the same pesky question at every meet. Of course, dressed as she was that evening in her stunning green Mysore silk with a royal golden zari border, a lovely pearl necklace and bangles, I would not blame the questioner for asking what she did! But somehow Ma's annoyance got the better of her, and with her characteristic sassiness she snapped: 'You have been wanting to know the secret of my youthfulness for so long now, isn't it? Hear it today.

Lung cancer, two heart attacks, two strokes, hypertension, extreme diabetes, glaucoma, neuropathy … The list is too long. Want to give it a try?' The poor lady didn't know what had hit her, and needless to say that evening I lost one of my top attendees.

Never have I seen Ma wearing make-up of any kind or going overboard to beautify herself. But our evening walks round the society complex would be preceded by a fifteen-minute ritual face-washing with generous splashes of cold water, applying a little moisturiser on her arms and face, tidying her hair and tying it up neatly, and finally changing into a comfortable, well-pressed salwar kameez. In my usual impatience I would sometimes urge: 'Can you please make it fast? No one down there is interested in seeing and admiring you!' With a stony gaze and matter-of-fact tone she would retort: 'I am not dressing up for someone else to admire me. I am making myself presentable so that I can feel good about myself!' Those words hit me now when I accidentally cross the mirror in her room that still has several of her bindis stuck to it.

When lost in endless worries and cascading thoughts, or just fiddling with my phone during our apartment walks or Bangalore's picturesque Lal Bagh gardens, she would quietly admonish me: 'Can you not live in the present for a change? Just soak in the beauty of what you see around? This fresh green leaf, that bright yellow flower, the breeze drifting over the lake, those chirping birds – can't you forget your mobile phone and just see, touch, hear, feel all of this instead of mourning the past or worrying about some unknown future?' These words ring in my ears when I'm sitting in her room, beaten and down, sometimes feeling absolutely helpless. It's like a whack from space telling me: Hey! Get up now! Enough of crying, get a grip on yourself and your life!

To love yourself, to find stability amidst your chaos, to make yourself feel good as well as those around you despite the traumas and travails you are going through is a rare and superhuman ability. Despite sharing the same DNA, I often feel envious of not inheriting this trait as much as it pulsed in her. It was, of course, so eerie that the universe fulfilled her wish to be presentable always, even when she departed. Prior to her birthday we had called the beautician for a home appointment, a birthday gift of a relaxing massage, facial, hair colour and pedicure-manicure pampering, a routine she succumbed to only once a year or so. When Ma lay in the icebox that day, her face was still bright and glowing. Mourners invariably commented that her peaceful, radiant face made one feel she would sit up at any moment and start fussing over her guests as she normally did. To leave in style and on your own terms is being quite obstinate with destiny too. And this for a woman who, given her fragile health, always feared that the end in some sanitised ICU ward might be painful and traumatic, featuring ventilators and pipes stuck into every pore. When I meet her on the other side the first thing that I'll tell her is this: 'Woman, do you even know how lucky you got?'

On many occasions, either during her frequent hospitalisation episodes or subsequent convalescence once back home, her closest friends from college days, Srilakshmi and Mamatha, came calling. In an instant this trio would become a raucous group of giggly teenagers. 'We've been the thickest of friends for close to fifty years now!' they would proudly proclaim, making me quite envious of them for not having such warm, intense friendships despite my best efforts, those bonds that stand the test of time. From bunking classes to see their favourite Dev Anand or Rajesh Khanna movies (by saving up bus fares given by their fathers), to mimicking their awkward chemistry professor in National College days, or the several mischiefs these otherwise innocent-looking girls would conjure for their unsuspecting victims. Seeing them laugh so joyously and revisit all those old life stories would light up my face. Like a fly on the wall, I'd quietly listen and laugh along as though I too had been a co-traveller in their film thriller. When I sit in Ma's room, I hear the echoes of boisterous laughter bursting forth from these three women as they remembered some random anecdote or a hapless victim of their harmless machinations. At some point in the entertainment Ma would realise she wasn't the wild teenager she thought she was, and that such vociferous laughter would stress out her weak lungs and heart.

One unfulfilled wish of hers was to go with her friends to a hill station resort that I was to book for her. Importantly, on this trip she wanted to try alcohol. 'How does wine taste? Is it very pungent? Is it like grape juice?' she questioned me innocently and insistently. Maybe the company of her best buddies would enhance the experience. Sadly, she left the world an alcohol virgin, her faltering health unable to permit the weekend getaway she so badly desired.

This non-complaining zest for life and finding pleasures in the smallest and most intricate of things, rather than waiting for big-bang celebrations, is something I have tried hard to acquire. 'You don't celebrate enough, Vikram!' she'd say. 'You've finished a difficult chapter in your new book? Come on, let's go for an ice cream to celebrate that. Celebration need not be only when something phenomenal happens! We can find happiness and celebrations in the smallest milestones too.' This, from a person who had a constant, gnawing pain in her chest and spine for nearly two decades, following the removal of half a lung, is a powerful life lesson I have been unable to learn. 'Celebration' also meant binge-watching utterly mindless television comedies like *Taarak Mehta Ka Ooltah Chashmah* or *Khichdi*. There she would be, all by herself, uncontrollably laughing at inane jokes, later insisting on narrating them to others, no matter how loudly they protested. Merriment came in small actions like whipping up a sweet *sanza* (semolina pudding) followed by refreshing green tea – usually at midnight when the two of us had the house to ourselves, my father having retired early to bed. Often there was no reason to celebrate beyond that we were alive and active.

Ma was a great lover of music. Though her family did not have the wherewithal to cultivate this keen interest, barring a brief dalliance with learning the veena, her artistic spirit never waned. While old Hindi film songs and ghazals were, of course, the all-time favourite, her interest in classical music was what she and Ajji, my maternal grandmother, passed on to me since a very tender age. With the crunched financial resources at our disposal in those years, when I look back, I realise what an unconditional sacrifice this must have been. There was no intent to make me a performing musician, and music was not a necessity for a family barely able to eke out a living. But only because precocious talent was seemingly noticed in her son who sang random jingles and bhajans with great fidelity and a clear voice, Ma went the extra mile to hone this in a proper, systematic way. Somewhere on the journey she also perhaps saw a consummation of her unfulfilled desire to learn music. As I began my vocal music lessons, rather reluctantly at the age of seven, Ajji and Ma would take turns to drop me to music class and wait. In between they would ensure I practised what I had learnt and that I took the art form seriously. With time, I was enraptured enough to grow without their goading.

From childhood Ma was my constant companion at endless concerts. 'You need to listen to more and more music to be able to learn it well,' she would say. Since 1939, with unbroken regularity until now, the Fort High School grounds of Bangalore came alive with several weeks of classical music performances commemorating Sri Rama Navami. In those open fields of makeshift tents and podiums made possible by the private efforts of connoisseur S.V. Narayanaswamy Rao, Bangaloreans feasted on the best music from across the country. The who's who and top maestros of Indian classical music performed with a sense of deep reverence for Lord Rama. The audience too became ecstatic co-passengers in that devotional journey. Ma would narrate tales to me of trips with her father as a kid.

Not being able to afford concert tickets, my grandfather came up with an ingenious solution. The venue's loudspeakers were sufficient to enjoy the music from outside. Once stationed by the gate they would gorge on groundnuts sold by a street-side hawker while swaying to the music. Perched on her father's shoulders was how Ma had seen, heard and enjoyed, albeit from afar, in sound and not sight, the likes of M.S. Subbulakshmi (whose concerts inevitably brought rain), M.L. Vasanthakumari, T. Chowdiah, Ustad Bade Ghulam Ali Khan, Siddheshwari Devi, Pt. Bhimsen Joshi, Dr M. Balamuralikrishna and other musical giants. When my interest in music began to bloom, Ma would insist on buying season tickets to these Fort High School concerts. The bus dropped us right outside the venue. All through the performance she kept watch, if I was keeping the taala, the beat, and if I had correctly guessed the raga being performed at any given moment. Our return bus trip saw us dissect aspects of the concert, making it such a wholesome learning experience for the budding student in me.

Even as I continued with advanced music lessons under eminent gurus, Ma ensured my interest was sustained and nourished. She was ever-ready to jump on the bandwagon with me to attend concerts, even when they were held at the other end of a traffic-ridden city like Bangalore, or went on through the night. She would insist on sitting with me sometimes when I practised, and if the tune or lyrics took an emotional turn, I saw tears streaming down her cheeks. She had her own favourites that she made a *farmayish* for in my practice sessions. Be it going all the way to Chennai to learn under Bombay Jayashri or staying closer to home in Bangalore under Dr Jayanthi Kumaresh and D.V. Nagaraj, Ma was my propulsion towards excellence. With her departure, the stream of music rippling joyfully through me has predictably dried. How does an ice-fed river flow when the glacier itself vanishes? My tanpura remains in her room, un-dusted, un-strummed. Yesterday I noticed that its strings had rusted since their last vibrations in January 2018. Every song, every raga, has so many memories associated with Ma that strumming the tanpura in her absence is not something I am brave enough to do.

Along with music, my parents cultivated the reading habit very early on. Being a socially awkward, shy, introverted single child, music and books became my constant childhood companions; they were the friends who would never abandon, bully or cheat me! Every time I excelled in exams my parents gifted me a book. Soon enough I had a vast library of priceless possessions. No doubt then that when my literary career began to flower, my parents – especially Ma – were the fountainhead of my creativity. In her youth she had learnt typing to supplement her income, taking odd part-time jobs after her work in the bank. Often, she would volunteer to type out chapters for my books, and could be relied upon to give harsh and critical feedback on whatever I was dictating. She was the most fastidious and difficult person to please.

When I became a published author, she sat in the first row of my public talks wearing a keen expression, watching every gesture, scrutinising the flow of words and my body language. Whatever praise or applause might come from the audience, my eyes always searched for her approval. Once home, there was usually a blow-by-blow debrief on where improvements could be made, such as: don't speak so fast, don't gobble up your words, use your hands better, maintain eye contact with everyone. This list was endless. But her simple tips and generous advice helped me to surmount a common obstacle in public speaking: stage fright. Ma was no consummate public speaker herself, and had never written anything for public consumption, her education not stretching beyond college graduation. Sheer commonsense coupled with unconditional love helped me navigate this new territory crowded with landmines and sharks. That I was controversy's favourite child disturbed her immensely. Several times she would make me vow not to talk or write about a certain subject that had the potential to ruffle feathers. Each time I stepped on stage or appeared in television debates, especially covering touchy, controversial subjects, her heart would skip a few beats – so she told me. But she would often tell her sister, 'Once the microphone is thrust in Vikram's hand and he starts speaking, some other power takes over and I relax.' With decades of public speaking under my belt, in every audience my eyes even now search in vain for the reassuring look, the approving smile, the glitter in the eyes (reserved for when I did my job well).

Despite the diabetes and daily insulin pricks, Ma was a passionate foodie. She also inherited from her mother a passion for cooking. Ajji, my grandmother, was a legendary cook. Friends and family travelled great distances to taste her specialties such as the famed *pooran polis*. Ma might be described as an egalitarian cook who went beyond Maharashtrian delicacies and experimented with new cuisines. An innovation of hers, the chocolate burfi containing generous dollops of butter, cocoa powder, dry fruits and nuts, was a sure-fire competitor to Cadbury and a runaway hit in my college hostel. Each time I arrived back at Pilani following vacations, hostel-mates and friends would ransack my luggage and disappear with the box of chocolate burfi! After the first experience, Ma began packing separate boxes for my friends. In my early hostel years at BITS Pilani as a homesick teenager, Ma would make solo trips in the middle of a semester. Travelling by train from Bangalore to Delhi, then enduring a horrendous bus ride from Delhi to Pilani in infamous Haryana Roadways buses, with bidi-smoking and puking passengers, Ma would cover her face fully with her dupatta and sit frozen for the six to seven hours of the tortuous ride. Once on campus, it was my friends who crowded round her more, to steal slices of her time, the maternal love and affection she exuded. Girls in my batch would purloin her for hours and without inhibition share their boyfriend problems and other worries, to which she appeared to always have a unique solution. 'She'd make such a good mother-in-law!' was their common refrain. Though, ironically, that was one thing Ma never became in her life.

Ma cherished the fine art of serving what she had cooked. Guests would be overfed to the brim but unable to stop smacking their lips at the culinary discoveries she had attempted. Those who relished every morsel or extended copious compliments were awarded with extra servings. During winters, the *avarekai* or hyacinth beans so unique to Bangalore were the object of her experimentation. From hot, crispy *kodubales* to *upma* and *akki rottis* made of *avarekai*, most of the neighbourhood would get to savour these trademark dishes.

When she wasn't in the mood for cooking, she sneaked out to eat out, especially spicy chaats, hot fluffy idlis, and crisp masala dosas. Her favourite joints in the city were the iconic Mavalli Tiffin Rooms (MTR), Vidyarthi Bhavan, or Taaza Thindi. During my short stint of working at Gurgaon, Ma visited me often to help me set up home. We would travel to Delhi, Agra, Mathura, and other nearby places where good food was a quintessential element. Although this may sound implausible, I have witnessed her tears of joy while munching on delectable papdi chaat and scrumptious golgappas in Gurgaon's Sector 14 market. Her last meal outside home was a birthday luncheon feast at her favourite MTR. Here the lunch is an elaborate ritual where scores of items are brought in quick succession by waiters, guaranteeing you will walk out tottering. 'This was the best meal I've ever had at MTR!' came her satisfied remark on her last birthday, two days prior to her sudden departure.

With a maniacal obsession for cleanliness, Ma always insisted that things needed to be in their place, neat and tidy, with not a speck of dust anywhere. This trait caused her to protest wildly when I insisted on having a dog at home. 'Choose between me and the dog!' she would say in jest. My reply would always be: 'Well, if that's the choice to make, you know for sure who's going to win – the dog, any day!' And we would laugh it away. Little did I know that this harmless banter was to come true perversely. Two months after her sudden departure, on the insistence of a friend who could not bear to see me sinking into a rabbit hole, a pet Labrador entered our lives to heal us from the tragedy. Ma perhaps sent Leo to heal the two silly men she had left behind in haste.

Even today her cupboard opens to a neatly arranged array of crisply-ironed saris. My mausi, her younger sister, tells me how each sari had a backstory, that many hardships had to be endured to save enough to buy a new sari, given their frugal means of survival. The cupboard still has the first sari that my father gifted before she married him, or the grander one she wore on her wedding day. The many other gifts my father and I showered on her when our family fortunes finally turned a tide are stacked up there with innumerable associated tales, secrets, little pleasures and soft tears, all quietly woven into the fabric and waiting to burst forth. Just that the one who valued them the most would never be there to feel their warm embrace.

Ever since her departure I have been ruminating constantly on the eternal, interminable bond between a mother and her child, even after one of them has departed.

I had a surreal experience of this a couple of years ago. At the height of the second wave of Covid in 2021, I was an unfortunate victim of the virus. My lungs had been completely infected and my heart affected. The doctors were doubtful about my survival prospects and told my family to prepare for the worst. That fateful night in the ICU when my heart began to collapse and a battery of doctors and nurses came running to resuscitate, I distinctly remember, even as I was slipping into unconsciousness, a bright apparition that stood behind the medical team. It was so clearly Ma whom I saw in the flashes of my near-death situation. There she was, standing right there with a gritty, tenacious look, commanding me not to give up, just as she had resolutely fought every illness she had faced. In the weeks of intense despair and soul-shattering isolation that followed, the comfort of a lingering maternal presence brought me back gently to life.

A couple of times, in a rather innocent manner Ma had challenged me: 'Why do you always write about these long-dead and forgotten people of the past? Write my biography! I have so much to share, many stories to tell the world. And for this, you don't even have to go out on strenuous research trips or rummage around dusty archives. You can just interview me and I will tell you everything!' I would mock her, saying: 'Huh! And who will read this book? Not even your husband!' The tinge of hurt and sadness in her eyes on hearing this remark would quickly fade and she would compose herself. This was no heightened sense of self-importance, but rather her way of wanting me to give her more of my time, more of my company, that my professional commitments and personal turmoil had deprived her of. To be able to just sit by her side, place my head in her lap as I did as a kid, hear these tales of her life while she gently ran her fingers through my hair – what I would not give for that!

When called upon to write this piece I was reminded of this conversation with Ma. Was she pulling strings from somewhere, making sure that at least some writing about her came out in print, if she couldn't yet have a full book?

Writing this personal story of my Ma has been a scary ordeal. Scary because, in the last five years I do not think I have deeply and honestly addressed my sense of immense loss. I have never articulated in spoken or written words what it meant to lose her. Like her embalmed room of objects and the saris in her cupboard, my unresolved emotions and feelings too were shut up inside, a carefully guarded closet.

The people we take as constants in our lives may be the very same we take too much for granted. They are seldom the ones we look up to in awe while they live, or think deeply about of their influences when we can tell them face to face. It was no different for me with Ma. For the first time, writing about what she meant to me has been a revelation. The beautiful life lessons she left behind through her own lived experience are what I had seldom reflected on intensely. We would happily lap up as great revelations the same principles, but couched in utter verbiage by some expensive spirituality or therapy sessions or self-help modules online. But when these principles come in unsophisticated, rustic words from a parent, and for free, they can seem less valuable, and so are less valued. Finding those little pleasures in life without any complaints, valuing our true, honest relationships, striving for a life that is a continuous joy rather than allowing it to be dominated by things that don't matter, are but a few things Ma taught me by example.

As I write, I keep looking at her photograph seated majestically on her bed. She would certainly not approve of freezing her room in the manner I have. 'Clean it all up right now. Change the bedspreads and pillow covers. Throw away that putrid water in the bottle!' I can almost hear her say. Maybe the best way to remember and emulate her is to dismantle the very object I hoped would capture her rich memory – this room. I realise that the 'object' that needs to remind me of her as well as my loss of her is not a bunch of physical artifacts. Instead, the person she was is to be found in her inspiring aura, her never-say-die spirit, and the many valuable lessons that make me whatever I am today. These things transcend the bricks and mortar of a room that has until now kept us both confined.

4

Love Letters

Jaishree Misra

Jaishree Misra has written eight novels published by Penguin and HarperCollins. She also edited an anthology, *Of Mothers and Others,* for Zubaan and Save the Children India. Her ninth book is a first-person account of the two years she spent trying to build a house on the beach in Kerala. She has worked in special needs, broadcast journalism and as a film classifier at the BBFC in the UK. www.jaishreemisra.com

'There comes a time in an ageing writer's life when it would seem more sensible to look up from one's desk and gaze outwards instead. I, therefore, teach English Communications to Vahani Scholarship students who fill up my diary and my heart. Having said that, it's very easy for editors to twist my arm as the urge to write is a madness that clearly doesn't simply disappear. I am glad for this writerly way to grieve the recent loss of my mum. Far better than wailing over her photo albums and letters, for what would the point be of that?'

Mahogany dressing table, Page 1 [Shashi Deshpande]

Iron house key, Page 21 [Devasiachan Benny]

The bed left untouched, Page 33 [Vikram Sampath]

Parents' wedding day, Page 61 [Jaishree Misra]

Brass bedchamber candlelight, Page 77 [Belinda RushJansen]

Blue Santa tie, Page 111 [Ramona Sen)

Wired electric lights, Page 125 [Sauma Afreen]

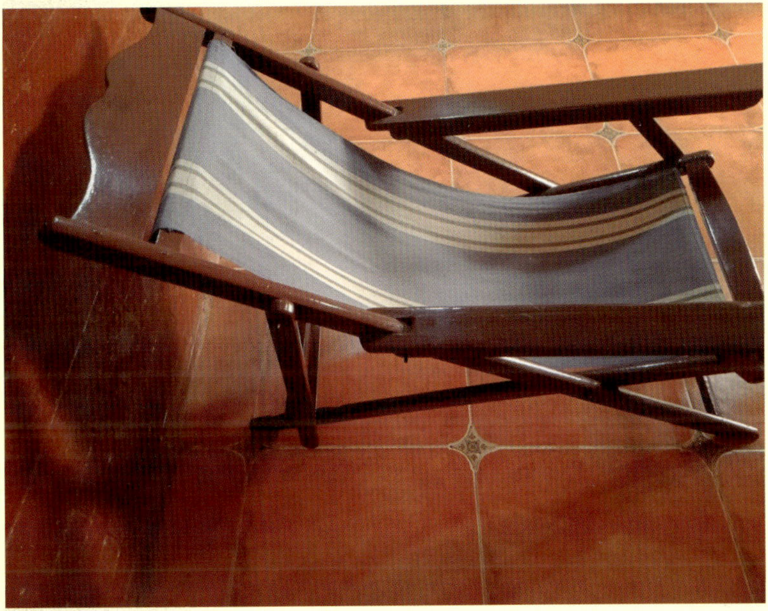

A dad's easy chair, Page 137 [Shinie Antony]

A father lost in music, Page 157 [Gajra Kottary]

The black-and-white snap was cloudy with age, the edges crumbling between my fingers. However, its subject (my parents) looked young and energetic, moving forward purposefully as though just about to step out of the picture and enter the room. Not dead any more, not suffering fatal heart attacks or trapped in the harsh ever-daylight of an ICU. But reborn as a vibrant and healthy young couple, about to start all over again.

They had been caught mid-action by a talented photographer as they walked around the temple that January day in 1959. It was a date that would subsequently be marked with Hallmark cards and cake for the next twenty-five years – and a pair of children pestering to be taken to a restaurant – but they would have been unaware of all that was to come, focused entirely on each other on this, their wedding day, as they held hands while walking the traditional parikrama around Guruvayur temple. Mum serene and beautiful and Dad beaming like a cat that was about to get the cream.

That is an accurate simile, as it happens. When I showed her the photo, my gossipy younger aunt immediately passed on the backstory. 'You know, your father wanted to skip the family do at Alleppey and go straight to Ooty with just her. Chechi told me.' I gasped, as the parents I had known were both extreme sticklers for rules. Plus, I had never seen them as libidinous exactly. 'Did they *do* that? Go to Ooty straight after the wedding?'

Auntie laughed. 'As if! Chechi knew Mummy would kill her if she did any such thing, so they obediently went to Alleppey. But they did get the Ooty trip. When they attended Thankappa chettan and Vasantha chechi's wedding a month later, they went together. All four went to Ooty.'

I tried not to look disgusted at the idea of my parents on a double honeymoon with another elderly couple. But there was more, as Auntie hadn't finished giggling her way through the rest of the story. 'Then you know what happened when they *reached* Ooty?' She was now laughing so hard, I thought she may not be able to finish the story. 'They found that the hotel had only booked one room!'

This was getting worse and worse. These parental lurches from exhibiting unseemly libido to planning a double-honeymoon to perhaps even indulging in a suggested orgy were most unsettling. 'So what did they do next?'

I enquired weakly. Auntie was in her element by now, pink-faced and wheezing. 'No problem! They took a sari and tied it across the room! One couple on the left, the other on the right!'

The chocolate tin full of old photos I had been going through did eventually reveal proof of that controversial Ooty trip too, sepia shots showing Mum and Aunty Vasantha as two elegant young Malayali women wearing coats over their saris, hair styled upwards in Fifties fashion. They looked so demure that my mind continued to boggle as I stared, hardly able to think of the pair indulging in hanky-panky with their respective husbands and nothing but a sari for separation.

I wondered if my parents' decorous wedding photos would ever again wear their previous air of incorruptible innocence. And how many more stories of derring-do lurked within this old Fry's tin with rusty edges?

My mother had often warned me. 'You will have to sort all of it out someday.' The statement was accompanied by an increasingly weary wave around her large and exceedingly cluttered home. She meant not merely these photographs but letters and files and bills, many of which went back thirty years to when she had bought this house after Daddy died. I had already spent a week ploughing my way through file after file containing mostly irrelevant papers: ancient Kerala Water Authority bills and Women's Club membership dues. I had also travelled down many a rabbit-hole, spending one especially nostalgic afternoon reading my own letters to Mum that charted the new life I was making for myself in the UK back in the 1990s. Every little scrap had been carefully filed.

But I had not bargained for suddenly becoming archivist to my parents' private life – papers and letters, revelations they had kept from their children. It should have helped that they actually loved each other but this had the rather curious effect of making me feel like a bumbling interloper, crashing about the delicate hinterland of their romantic association that lay far from the mundane domesticity I was more familiar with, and very definitely more comfortable with.

Perhaps these were not intended to be secret but merely signalled the kind of diffident approach Mum specialised in. Wasn't it faintly distasteful to parade one's happiness before the world when not everyone was equally blessed? My parents did not even think they should indulge in public displays of affection in front of their children, for who knew what effect this would have on young minds (when I was a teenager, Mum lived in constant fear of me losing my virginity, for one). I, therefore, have not one recollection of Mum and Dad cuddling on the sofa or holding hands. At best, I can claim to have seen them exchange a glance across a crowded room, signalling time to leave a party. Or the odd occasion when Dad would place his hand on the small of Mum's back as they left a room together. But that was it. And hence the shock of coming across an innocuous paper bag stuffed with written declarations of love, some in card form, others in now tattered inland letters. What was I to do with this private cache that belonged firmly to another world and to two people who would almost certainly not want me feasting my eyes on it.

It soon became clear that Mum had determinedly kept secret not just their love but also the extent to which she had mourned Dad after he had gone. He had died very unexpectedly of a heart attack that had taken all of five minutes at the untimely age of fifty-seven. Mum (herself just fifty) had been devastated of course. That was no surprise. Everyone knew what a devoted couple they had been. But then, with typical quiet tranquillity, she reinvented herself, moving back to Kerala and becoming once again the small-town girl she had always been while eschewing the glamorous Air Force life she had excelled at alongside my father when he had been alive.

That had been that, as far as most of us knew. Mum had overcome her grief with typical consideration for the feelings of those around her and got on with the rest of her life. She had had another thirty-eight years, in fact, a widowhood that turned out to be longer than her twenty-five years of marriage. Only very occasionally did she slip into mild self-pity, mentioning the number of years she had managed 'without him' and lamenting that, while he had provided well for her in terms of property and pension, he himself had enjoyed so little of it.

Early in 1987, Mum, now eighty-seven, emerged from her bathroom to get ready for bed after an evening of TV viewing. The maid reported later that her eyes were still on the screen, hooked as she was on the storyline of *Koodevide*. And that was when she tripped and fell against the footboard of her own bed. It took me a long time to look at that bed without imagining her crashing down on it, breaking seven ribs and causing an unstoppable bleed in her brain. It took another month in hospital before she eventually died, each day leaching a little more of our hope. Sitting by what I knew was her deathbed, I took to whispering reminders that Daddy awaited her somewhere beyond. But I doubt she heard me and, even if she had, she was pragmatic enough to know that it was mere fancy to imagine reuniting romantically with the great love of her life who had departed all of thirty-eight years ago. Even I, far more given to quixotic flights of fancy, couldn't quite square up the meeting in an afterlife of my fifty-seven-year-old father with the eighty-seven-year-old Mum had become.

It fell on me, her only daughter and the person who was to inherit her house in Trivandrum, to go back at some point and 'sort things out', just as she had warned. I considered myself good at that sort of thing, terrier-like in my tendency to hang grimly on until I had finished a task. But, when I moved into Mum's house and started living her life by default, with only her night maid to keep me company, I found myself sucked into a strange vortex where time had moved backwards and I was in some curious way becoming my mother. Is that where those nocturnal dreams emerged from? Fevered sequences, sometimes sepia-tinged, in which I either saw or was my young mother smiling and bending her ear towards my father while he whispered naughty utterances about all the things he intended doing to her in Ooty.

Sleeping in her house so soon after her death was oddly comforting. But living her life played strange tricks on my mind. I had not expected to actually feel her girlish early infatuation for a man in uniform. Nor had I realised that, leafing through her recipe books, I would actually taste the fancy party dishes she cooked for those big Air Force shindigs pulled off with such élan. There was also the day I found her 'England album', which set me off, sailing on *SS Iberia* with my young family, feeling the cold winds of the Atlantic whip through my sari.

Most of her life with Dad had probably been lots of fun, but she had not talked about that life for years. My blithe assumption had been that she had swiftly come to terms with her fate of an early widowhood and simply moved on, but I was now consumed with guilt for failing to consider the loneliness she must have felt evening after evening after evening. She had not voiced her pain, which gave everyone permission to assume she had not felt much. It was only her death and the odd carrier bag of memories that laid bare the secrets she wouldn't have dreamt of burdening anyone with while she was alive.

It was finding Dad's pocket diary tucked away deep inside her cupboard that finally undid me: 1985, the cover said, the year he had died. It was all there, in his typical neat jottings and in almost exactly the same fashion I maintain my diaries today. Little notes to self (check railway booking, collect number plate, meter reading 01915), reminders of things to buy (peanut butter, inland letters). And, finally, the day he died when everything seemed to go as planned until the clock stopped at noon. Not in his diary, though, as he had made entries for the following few days too: a niece's wedding to attend, a planned trip to Calcutta for an Aeronautical Society symposium ... Life was meant to carry on, unending.

How often had Mum taken out this little diary and pored over it in the days after his death, searching for some hint of a goodbye, maybe a bit of salve for her pain? If there was comfort to be had, she had clearly reserved it for her most private moments.

I slipped the diary in amongst the letters and tied the top of the carrier bag in a double knot. In the backyard, the domestic help had built a bonfire of old bank statements whose flames were now leaping high. Nobody noticed as I slipped the last evidence of my parents' love into the fire. Some lovers wish for public declarations, others for memorials and towers in the sky. But my parents weren't like that at all. It seemed to suffice that they had enjoyed a steady and nourishing love for twenty-five years. For some that is enough.

5

The Brass Candlestick

Belinda RushJansen

Belinda RushJansen has exhibited at the Royal Society of Arts in Edinburgh, where she was awarded Best Female Sculptor in 1996. She studied sculpture at Edinburgh College of Art, graduating in 1983, and currently works in English alabaster, Cornish soapstone, bronze and found materials. Her pieces, ranging from hand-held carved memory stones to life-sized barbed-wire cattle, are shown in public and private collections across the world.

'From my beginnings in London, then many moves further and further north in Scotland, thanks to my mother my life was marinaded in animals, and the wild landscapes became my inner sanctuary, supporting me through all the trials of existence. My work and life are inspired by the profound teachings that nature provides.'

Cosy by my wood burner at Honeypot cottage in the absolute quiet of a dark winter's night I watch the reflection of metal and flame in the black glass beyond.

The brass chamber candlestick with its finger loop to carry and light you to bed holds the history of known and unknown people. Its last owner was my mother. It is one of only two of her infinity possessions I have in my life.

My mother is held in a sepia photo at arm's-length, sitting on her mother's knee in the Paris of 1918. Her mother, a Quaker and WWI nurse, has with her a young husband, swiftly promoted to Major in the trenches as the sole survivor bar one of his Company. His wife, my Yorkshire Quaker grandmother, is tall, slim and fair, and looking a little shocked at this dark-haired, very present, robust baby girl who takes after her husband's French side.

A rich tapestry of life rolls out for this baby who becomes my mother in 1960, a very different era from 1918.

I am her third and late child by a second husband that she tries to rescue from his childhood war trauma.

My mother was an unusual woman, a powerful helper of others and exceptionally strident in taking on good causes. Unable to cope with my father, she took who she was then and my four-year-old self far away from our Hampstead home to a series of untraceable homes across Scotland. Each home displaying varying degrees of dereliction, she impressively renovated while holding down senior psychiatric social work jobs in the main Scottish hospitals.

Living alone as a full-time working mother, no sister and mother to help as with her first two children (now away at Quaker boarding school), she was faced with parenting an introverted and bereft stubborn small daughter who could not understand where her much-loved father had vanished to. As consolation, animals were lavished on me, which became my companions. To keep the animals happy and also to keep me hidden from my father, who she was convinced would abduct me to Holland and his family, she moved us through a variety of landscapes, yo-yoing between large-gardened houses in town where we tried to corral our ever-expanding pet families, and back out to the wilderness, away from complaining neighbours.

The wilds were a romantic idea for her, but not her natural place after a London childhood and a very glamorous Oxford college-girl life with a brief disastrous attempt at being a land girl in the War. She had lived in the wilds of Sudan with her first District Commissioner husband and was game by nature, but the Scottish climate, damp homes and many life challenges easily gave her flu and pneumonia. We lived on the move every two years, from town to country to moors to mountains to valleys to marshes by sea bays and forests. Our menagerie in tow.

The brass candlestick most reminds me of the farmhouse on the moors in winter when I was seven. This was our first truly wild home. As I stepped out of the car and stretched, the man handing over the door keys remarked to my mother that I looked like an animal released from a cage. And the candlestick, always packed somewhere in our possessions, carried the strong presence of our last but one croft home in the Black Isle as a teenager. It's an object that reminds me of winter nights, of generators and power cuts, of tumultuous storms and horizontal rain hitting the thin bedroom window like chucked gravel. Of smoky wood fires and bedtimes looking up at inked skies pinpricked with stars. Back when I was seven in the farmhouse on the moors, there I would stand under the vastness of the thin, cold air, waiting for the dogs to hopefully have a last piddle before sleep.

Held high, the candlestick lighted the long corridors with flickering shadows that travelled with me between bathroom and bedroom in that lonesome farmhouse. It reminds me of playing with the melting wax and the warmth of a fire on my back when the countryside is iron-hard cold and the lake deep-frozen. It reminds me of being too scared to sleep in my own bed and creeping into my mother's big bed festooned with her tiny Chihuahuas too small to live alongside the big kitchen dogs – the Pharaoh hound, the Alsatian, the Afghan hound, Whippets, the Ibizan hound, the Shelties and many other dogs that came and went. The big dogs had an enormous sofa downstairs to sleep on. The Chihuahuas upstairs lay snuggled like snails in every crevice of bedding, rising in a sea swell as I eased myself under the covers next to them, safe behind the comforting mass of my mother's soft sleeping body, the paperweights of little snoring dogs upon me. All in together, the bluish light of a television (which she would fall asleep in front of nightly) glowed over her multifarious possessions that bulged and half-escaped from un-closable drawers and cupboards bought in auctions.

One drawer contained half-stale digestive biscuits (to share with the dogs) and a small glass whisky bottle shaped like a hip flask sporting a picture of a grouse –

her medicinal nightcap with hot orange and honey; I can smell it still. A radio that worked and several that didn't, an alarm clock similarly so, a glass of water with false teeth, pale dusty face powder with a fluffy powder puff pad balanced half-off-half-on the rim of its cut-glass jar, a deep sticky red lipstick uncovered in its shiny golden tube, nail scissors and a file, a split bag of Glacier mints with polar bears drawn on each blue wrapper, a hairbrush invariably full of hair, odd lost earrings, an Exchange and Mart paper bent open on the pets and livestock page, the *TV Times* magazine and many other half-wanted items. On the floor, yesterday's local paper spread out sent wafts of dog piddle, dissolving the newsprint into the stuffy bedroom air. Next to the papers were propped-opened suitcases, always part-unpacked and ready for the next move. One such case housed a large fluffy cat that lovingly draped itself across my mother's clothes. Hand-raised as a kitten by her on Carnation milk, this orphan grew equally magnificent in physical dimensions and adoration for my mother. Sometimes hearing her on the telephone in the stairwell below, the cat would fling himself onto her thick head of hair, remembering the way she had kept it warm and enabled its survival from tiny kitten-hood beginnings. My mother, jumpy at the best of times, would scream and protest, but nothing would put him off.

Our six o'clock mornings still dark in winter, an Aga-warmed kitchen dispensing breakfast to our assorted dogs and cats, my parrot and tropical fish, on with the scarf hat and boots and out to the yard to feed the hens and geese and ducks and pet turkey and rabbit. A breakfast of hot porridge, then the long rough-track drive with dawn breaking. A late drop to a school playground empty of children, already ensconced with their books, my mother would race off to her hospital work taking a dog or two with puppies into the office. As I grew old enough to be left at home with the animals I began to find ways to persuade my hard-pressed mother to agree to giving me the immense freedom of my preferred animal companions, of unbound days exploring nature, things that remain vital to me today.

Given the many never unpacked suitcases, thirty years later it took time to clear out my mother's final home. I found her own mother's handbag, glasses and false teeth, and at the back of a bedside drawer a small handgun. I will never know who the gun belonged to, but I think perhaps the candlestick was my mother's mother's, and perhaps its being handed on to me has more connection than I can know.

The brass candlestick sits on my window table. I place in its holder only the purest off-white candles my cousin makes.

The almost ritualistic lighting of the wick as winter nights draw in brings a meditative solace. My evenings are quiet with no telly and no drawn curtains, just the quiet draw of a fire, and beyond the large dark window the nature reserve where owls can be heard and sometimes the bark of a deer or the shrieks of foxes.

When my young grandson comes to stay it is for him to light the candle and watch the curling smoke of the extinguished match. This treasured brass object holding its candle continues to light the way from generation to generation.

6

What Happened To P'ecious

Jerry Pinto

Jerry Pinto is a poet, writer, translator and editor. He poetises, writes, translates and edits in a city by the sea. He has lost count of the number of times he has tried to describe himself but remembers well the number of times he has succeeded in writing one of these paragraphs that has any resemblance to himself: none.

'Loss is an inherent part of human existence. We lose time as we gain experience. We lose the chance to gain experience if we choose only to spend time. In our losses are our gains. In all that we gain, someone else loses. Life takes on some peculiar shapes and losses are formative forces.'

Missing: round-headed, dot-eyed, cloth figure with stumpy legs and long prehensile arms. Does not answer to the name P'ecious.

I have to say that things don't disappear in the way that people do. People go. They walk away. They run. Sometimes they are running from situations and circumstances or so they say. But in truth, they are always running away from people. Some are running from other people, some are running from themselves. They could be running to someone too. That is what people do. Things don't. Things stay. Things are.

I am a thing in that strange category that human beings have invented: the homunculus. Not satisfied with the number of people they have around them, they create other variants, variants without life: dolls, fetishes, totems, images, deities, statues, paintings ... the list is endless. They give them names: Madonna, Lucifer, Banshee, Chudail, Anansi. Read the list aloud and watch your mind. See how it responds.

Let each one come into focus and you will see that each one trips a switch. Something goes off. Breast, fire, scream, cheat, trickery. What are you thinking? How are you thinking? Are you looking for a way to link all these together? Are you scanning the horizon for a sign? Are you cheating by looking at the end before the beginning? Are you blinking in disbelief?

I am a thing.

Then I was not.

For I did an un-thing-like thing.

I vanished.

There were two of them. They were happy children generally and in specific ways too. They loved stories and for a long while, they told each other stories, inventing endlessly, knitting and patching and stitching together bits of old stories with new ones, things heard and things thought, things that were real and things only imagined. And they peopled this world, they staged it for each other and for themselves. The hot afternoons melted away in dialogue and character development. Stories were postponed and revisited and improved upon.

For all this, they needed dolls.

Sometimes the dolls could be crowd-fillers, if the story was a romance. Sometimes, things could be incorporated, things that were not human but given human natures. When their father bought a new black umbrella with a mahogany handle and their mother found herself in possession of a red floral folding umbrella, the black brolly became Jonathon and the red one, Parizaad. The whole thing ended in a dance sequence: Jonathon grave and sedate, turning once or twice as Parizaad pirouetted and spun, her frill fluttering.

Everything in that house could be named, would be named. Some names stuck, others changed with the sound of music in their mouths. Ms Favre Leuba told the time.

Child 1: Who gets their name from their face?

Child 2: She has a tattoo because her elder sister got lost in a fair.

Child 1: So how is having her name on her face going to stop her from getting lost in a fair?

Child 2: You'll have to ask her father.

Child 1: Who is her father?

Child 2: I don't know but her father's father is a…

Child 1: … a grandfather clock.

They talked endlessly, these children. They talked for themselves and they talked for all those who had been named. They talked for plates.

Child 1: Don't scrape me with the side of your spoon.

Child 2: It wasn't me, it was the fork.

Child 1: Oh, fork.

Child 2: Gigigigigigigigi.

Parent: Eat your food now.

They talked for the plush red rabbit, the white fur rabbit, the gold-eared dog, the pink teddy bear and the brown teddy bear.

They made up voices. They gave them characters. They invented backstories.

Their parents bought them more. Their parents' friends bought them more.

I once counted eighteen of them with original names. Names that had been argued and discussed, names which had been changed and reinvented.

I had a borrowed name.

Child 1 had a grandmother. (By the time Child 2 came along, the grandmother was a thing, a dead thing.) Child 1's grandmother thought Child 1 was precious, so precious that she had to cut some prickling out of the word precious and render it softer, smoother, silkier; she made it p'ecious. Child 2 took that word, put a capital letter on it and gave it to me as a name.

When an umbrella becomes Jonathon, he has a square jaw and shoulders. When another umbrella is called Parizaad, she acquires a tip-tilted nose and an arched instep. The names faded after a while and they went back to being umbrellas. As umbrellas, they got left behind.

My name was dust. It settled on me. It blew in through a window and it settled on me.

So maybe I was wrong.

Maybe things go too.

But we don't move. We flatten slowly. Dust will tell you the story. I know dust. I understand it. Human beings like to say that they are made of stardust. They are but so is everything else. Everything else. Kites and kayaks, pygmy shrews and pelicans, durians and dodos, honey and urine, everything.

Me too.

Stardust in my eyes watching dust. It blows in through the open windows. It sloughs off the warm vibrant bodies of Child 1 and Child 2. It hovers. It asks for water vapour and gets it and turns into clouds. It flirts with air currents, it rides thermals, it coheres, it gains in size and gravitas and gravity, it settles. A dot here, a dit there, a bit here, a tot there, dit-dot-bit-tot-dit-dit-dot-bit-bit-bit-tot…

First, dust is a discolouration. It is a spatter. Then a work of incidental, accidental art, a pointillist work of art by stardust. Then dust becomes a re-colouration. What is the colour of dust? Dust is dusty, dust-coloured. Dust is the colour of defeat. Dust is a declaration of disinterest. To reclaim a space, dust must be dispelled. It retreats but it will return. Human beings have been warned. Dust thou art and unto dust thou shall return. So terrified by this they invented the soul: 'Dust thou art to dust returnest/ Was not spoken of thy soul.' They wage war against dust, sweeping, wiping, dusting, vacuuming.

What use is that? I often wonder. Dust will win. Dust will always win. Dust has been here long before anyone of us was even a dream. Dust will be here long after we cease to haunt anyone's dreams. To fight dust, however, is easy. You have to care. You have to care enough to move. Movement does not allow dust a temporary victory.

Movement, for a thing, depends on the kindness of the living world so you can see how hopeless that is. Of your kindness, give me an adult. But of course, this is not possible. I have been designed for another world, the savage world of the child. Here, nothing counts as much as the warmth generated by a thing. It is a strange internal warmth. It arises in the stewpot of the heart and in the chamber pot of the mind. Welcome to childhood, the ultimate 'hood.

And before you grow sentimental at the innocence of children, let me point out that even Saint Augustine of Hippo, church father and scholar, pointed out: The weakness of infant limbs, not its will, that is its innocence. In the grip of a child, I have often wondered whether toys were not invented that children might do unto others what has been done unto them. I have been hurt, the child says inside the stewpot, I have been senselessly hurt. The chamber pot echoes: It is now my turn to senselessly hurt. And off comes the head of the doll. When the child cries afterwards, it is not because it regrets this action; it is because there are unjust consequences. My mother hurt me but I am here. I hurt you and I demand that you should be here so that I might hurt you again just as I will be available to her so that she may hurt me again. How dare you die? How dare you fall apart? How dare you not scream?

I am lucky that way. I am all of a piece, a single piece, and in order to decapitate me you would need a pair of sharp scissors or a knife. And a child given those is likely to put them to even better use – to hurt its own person or to draw real blood rather than the cotton with which I am stuffed.

You are now impatient with any philosophising. You want to know what happened to me.

You remember the evening Marcelline visited the house? Marcelline, the woman who used to clean it years ago? She came to invite your family to her eldest daughter's wedding and she brought her youngest child, Sihon, along?

You saw him only in passing, hanging at an angle to her, reluctance personified. You did not pause because you had things to do and places to go. You did not see them leave, for you would have seen me dangling from Sihon's hand at the same angle that he dangled from Marcelline's arm. I moved, I was moved and the dust fell off me.

Yes.

He took me.

Marcelline was not the kind to look at her child. She had his hand in hers and so she knew the rest of him was following a couple of whiny steps behind. If she had seen what he had done, she would have given him two tight slaps, which would have scarred him for life and made him into an alcoholic in due course. But she did not notice because when he got home, I was plucked out of his hand by Veronica, his sister, who knew that Mummy would help herself to the tea and the sugar but did not think of that as stealing. Veronica understood without being able to enunciate the rule: it is only stealing if it will be missed. A stuffed toy will be missed but five tablespoons of tea leaves wrapped in a handkerchief will not. Marcelline would have brought me back and my story would have continued to be the story of dust instead of the story of an absence.

But Marcelline did not notice and you did not notice either though I must have left some mark of my absence behind, at least a tracing, an outline where I had protected the surface beneath me from the setting of the dust.

And so there was no reason for me to return, was there?

Was there?

I could say I was deeply loved but I was not. I could say I participated in a million imaginary games. I could say I became family. I could say anything and you would believe me.

Instead, I became a friend.

Sihon was a quiet child, and he had many plans in his head. He wanted to paint, he told me, and that was because he liked colour more than anything in the world. He could not see purple without feeling hungry. He could not see green without wanting to cry. When he was young, the feelings came in savage bursts but he learned slowly to control them; or perhaps the colours became easier to see, or maybe his skin grew thicker. This happens to children, so Picasso says.

Sihon talked to me about colour. He could not tell anyone else in his world about it. The boys would have called him names, his family would have thought this a waste of time. My silence was my listening. He told me about a hibiscus in the church graveyard and the flame of its maroon heart and how it got the name shoeflower from its blackness when crushed. He told me about the hot brown of bread at the baker and how it made him quiet and alone inside his head even when he was outside. He told me about how moss-green walls were a glittering invitation to walk in jungles, and stars stuck in the cement made him feel empty and hollow, and how Teacher Lidwin's curtains made him want to jump down somewhere because there was a small pond in that colour, a small pond in a garden with a turtle that lived at the bottom.

Who do you talk to about this? Who can you talk to about the wildness of colour, the intensity of it? When Sihon smoked his first joint, he told me the truth about purple. He said that he had asked himself to swallow his eyeballs. And so he went down into his stomach, the red of a volcano, the chyme as lava, so hot it was white, so white hot and so much, so overwhelming that even a brain swollen with the effects of pot could not handle it, but there was blue, a sedate blue vein into which he merged. I loved this description as much as I hated it. My own interiority was undifferentiated matt fibre: white coarse with a few dead black nodes, seeds that had remained, desiccated now and drained of life. (I hated it because I was of my time and did not trust what these drugs could do to Sihon's head.) In the vein he understood purple.

Purple is the colour of blood in the secrecy of the body. It is red and maroon and incarnadine and rubious in the air when its secrets are exposed to light. Purple is life, he said to me.

I said: Colour is life.

He saw that I meant it. He looked me over, my pale out-coloured body, my black mark face, and saw through me to my pallid insides. He saw how I was destined for lifelessness because I had no colour and he was sad and he felt each colour inside his body as life. He saw that I spoke as a prophet from a desert about a tropical rainforest. My colourlessness, my pallidity, my wan blanched face had offered me a clear space to see what I did not have and would never have.

In that moment our connection became real. He began to read about colour, the physics of it. Colours as a rejection of bandwidth. Colour as the stain on a surface. Colour as temperamental as a human being's gaze. Colour as individual. Colour as a beatitude of nature.

I like to think I saved him colour for colour. He could fill my ears with tales of colour, some colourful, some as boring as discussions of theoretical matters. To whom else could he speak?

In college he told me about refraction and the spectrum and later about Goethe and Yves Klein. He joined the Max Mueller Library and read Goethe on colour. There was much in this to think about and much I did not understand, but eventually Sihon became an expert in colour and went to work in New York at a museum where he wrote many important research papers.

Eventually he wrote a paper about purple – he held his tongue about the secrets of blood, for which I could only be glad. There are some things you should only tell things. He won his place in a colour laboratory. He left the marsh areas of Mahim and tried to take Marcelline with him but she found it hard outside her parish, her tenement, her world, so he let her go home. But he brought me with him to New York.

I sit by his bedside. Most days he says nothing to me but in the night, he pats me on the head and says, 'Don't be afraid. All the colour will come back in the morning.'

Good night, I say, good night.

7

Tie-ing Up The Blues

Ramona Sen

Ramona Sen's latest novel, *The Lady on the Horse and Other Secrets*, has been published in India by Speaking Tiger Books in 2024. Her first novel, *Crème Brûlée*, was published by Rupa Publications. She has also been an editor with HarperCollins India and a reporter with *The Telegraph India*. Her musings on food have been published by *My Kolkata* (*The Telegraph*), *Borderless Journal*, *The Bangalore Review*, as well as in the collection of essays, *The Moving Finger*. She is one of the founders of the content and communications company, Allcap Communications.

'We have arrived at a day and age where a tie is considered too stiff to be fun. Ties are now for gruelling meetings or tiresome formal interactions. For my dad, a tie was a winter accessory to be carefully selected for the suit of the day, to accurately reflect the mood of an occasion. I find myself judging a tie by what he might have thought of it. Reflecting on this has enabled me to pause and recall our best times together.'

It's Christmas day. Jim Reeves's smooth-as-brandy-sauce voice sighs in the background that he is dreaming of a white Christmas. There is half a plum cake under the cloche on the dining table, the other half having been demolished at breakfast. The antique silver angel, holding two slender candles, stands upright on the sideboard while the artificial tree is askew in its brass tub on the landing. We are tripping over each other, trying to get ready for Christmas lunch. Everything is as it usually is.

Here I am, in my bedroom, standing in front of the mirror trying to manoeuvre your Santa tie into a perfect four-in-hand – I don't have the patience to attempt anything more than the simplest knot, even though I've watched you display a perfect Windsor every morning of winter. I turn on a video to follow a demonstration for making the loop. I tug more carefully. I wouldn't need advice if you were here. On the other hand, if you were here, I would be wearing my Santa brooch on a dress, and you the Santa tie with your grey suit, the cerulean blue pocket square a dignified contrast to a bright red sled. It is the only day in the year you would acquiesce to sporting a greeting-card tie. Christmas always made you jolly, like a wobbly tipsy pudding. It's the nip in the air, it's the sizzling steaks, it's the midnight mezzo-soprano reverberating through the cathedral.

It's especially hard to believe that you're no longer here for Christmas.

Your regular ties still droop from the neat rack inside the cupboard door – cobalt with paisley, indigo with minuscule polka dots, that azure with hairline stripes. When the seasons began to turn, when warm October nights were melting into cool November mornings, out would come the coat brush to demonstrate the removal of dandruff-white lint with brisk, light strokes. Winter dressing was an elaborate affair interleaved with lessons on how many inches of shirt cuff should be visible under a coat sleeve (never more than half an inch), and whether it is permissible to wear brown shoes with light grey pants (it is, but oxblood is better). Most importantly, I learned how to preserve the drape of a coat by sliding into it seamlessly without struggling through the arms. This required me – your young valet on duty when not at school – to stand on a stool and stretch to hold the coat above her head so that you could slip into it just *so*. If that isn't a morning well spent with your daughter, we don't know what is. You shook my hand solemnly, picked up your russet, brass-buckled briefcase and headed out, delighted that the season to dress for work had finally arrived. I knew it was to be a long, important day when a crest-emblazoned tie was selected to accompany a crisp white shirt. While jaunting off in a plain ol' polka-dotted tie meant you'd have time to pick up kebabs for dinner, that we'd watch a Hitchcock classic and I'd listen out for comments on the shade of Cary Grant's tie.

There were ties for all seasons and all reasons.

Respectful white stripes on navy blue softened the ire of teachers exasperated by my poor grades and last-row truancy. 'We are sure she could do better,' they would say, reining in the 'she's lazy and simply won't study'. This particular tie looked more apologetic than I felt, but you would take me out for lunch anyway. Intent on using ham sandwiches to convince me it might be worth a shot to pass algebra and organic chemistry, you didn't notice the tie veering towards the tartar sauce, causing me to giggle and inducing you to look down and exclaim impatiently – not least because of the need to explain to my mother why, in spite of the poor grades, you had taken me out for a hearty meal. I would attempt to wipe off the sauce with a napkin and warm water. I revelled in our unspoken agreement that there would be no mention of the lunch when we reached home.

Perhaps the reason you had such a well-stocked tie rack was because so many gravitated towards the saucière. During Sunday dinner the periwinkle paisleys found their way into the chocolate sauce waiting to be dribbled over ice cream. You couldn't keep the silver polka dots far enough from the gravy boats at winter wedding buffets. Your blue-grey shadow stripes developed a penchant for cream of mushroom soup. Some of these stained ties found an alternative career as props for school stage antics, where the costumes for storytelling butler, unfaithful husband, Tobermory the Cat were enhanced by ties containing evidence of a colourful past.

My father's blues ruined me for the mauves, corals and ambers I would encounter as an independent young woman. When I stepped from a Catholic girls' school into the red-blooded world, it was with stunned disbelief that I realised boys are just ordinary beings, that not all of them followed my childhood rulebook. There was nothing like a tie bursting with orange flames to ruin a date, where attempts to suppress a reaction ended up with me choking on the fries. I spent whole evenings willing a red polka-dotted tie to turn back into the dress this fabric surely must have been created for. A well-meaning friend informed me that a luminous aquamarine was no reason to let a nice boy go. Blast it, I thought, I will wear my own ties. Your ties. Between us, we could manage a new shade of blue to the office every day of winter.

Surrounded by people who knew you as well as you allowed them to, I recall how an unwillingness to give way to excessive merriment was sometimes eroded by a half-smile hovering on your lips. And although often solemn, you found a way to see the lighter side of life at unexpected moments, diffusing someone's ill-disposition with a droll one-liner. I recall lessons in temperance as I slip into blue leather Mary Janes that you would have approved of, even while my mood oscillates with the vagaries of an aggravating day.

Our shared proclivity for chic winterwear did not, in fact, make me a chip off the old block, or a thread of the old tie, as the case may be. Perhaps I wasn't sufficiently attentive to your tutelage while buttoning those cardboard-stiff cuffs. I choose to flout the house rules, sitting cross-legged at the table. I wear running shoes to work, and even though I remember your advice to 'err on the side of caution', I've erred on the side of reckless more times than you would have approved of. And although you impressed upon me the importance of remaining stoic through loss and luck, to avoid the pitfalls of excess and exuberance, I saw that misadventures can shape us too. I try to find the courage to unwrap my heart for at least some to see. In seeking to understand myself, I wonder all the more about what your greatest trials might have been, if you found fatherhood mostly joyous or troublesome, whether you arranged your life as carefully as a tie rack, the external order masking an inner life no one else was privy to. For you remained dapper and inscrutable until the end.

That stroke took you before I learnt to tie a schoolgirl knot. You were gone before I could frame important questions I wanted to ask instead of debating why pizza was deemed unacceptable for breakfast or why we couldn't catch a night show at the new multiplex.

We put you in a new suit, selecting a sombre navy tie with tear-blue stripes for your final winter outfit. The other mourners, waiting to burn their own dead, didn't believe ties belonged in a crematorium, muttering that suits were more appropriate for a coffin at a graveyard. Nevertheless, we let the ashes fall into the cloudy river. Sometime later we brightened the house with a powder blue paint – a shade you would have liked very much, not least because it sharpened the contrast to the red brick façade.

On winter days the neighbourhood odd-job man still wears your old maroon cardigan. When asked if there was something he wanted as a memento, he chose this piece of clothing. The only time I saw his weather-beaten face crumple in grief was the day he watched you being driven away for the final rites, wrapped in white, encased in glass. You were, after all, supporting his efforts to move out of a shanty in the marketplace to live in a bricks-and-mortar house. I rarely heard you mention the many people who turned to you in difficult times, but they didn't fail to turn up to your rain-washed memorial. Of course, you never talked about the times you might have needed help, that heart of yours concealed behind beautifully tailored suits. And now I realise that to err on the side of caution also means to present oneself with moderation, where acts of generosity are executed without fanfare so that the world cannot foil either formality or best intentions.

A decade later, the neat tie rack has returned to its usual self. Although we tried, our dupattas and scarves never quite belonged in your orderly cupboard, or the skinny jeans and palazzos for that matter. Christmas day has come round again, and following a tradition of my own I retrieve the jolliest of all the ties displayed behind the door. I eke out the moments before lunch begins without you, I pause over the reds on the greeting cards received this year, costumes for carollers, berries on holly, ribbons for handbells, bright festoons round a tree. I walk downstairs promising to keep the ends of your Santa tie well away from the brandy sauce. All in all, it's going to be another merry blue Christmas.

8

Lanterns

Sauma Afreen

Sauma Afreen has a BA and an MA in Arts in English and a BA in Education from Aligarh Muslim University. A recipient of the Shoa Fatima Memorial Award, she freelances as an Alt Text Writer with Scribblers-and-Scribes and was creative workshop mentor and writer on the Sadabahar project for Artificial Silk (UK Shared Prosperity Fund). She was awarded mentorship on the LEDBy Accelerator Program 2022 and previously interned with NGO Pocketful of Sunshine, which prevents child abuse, writing an article about her experience: https://pfosunshineindia.com/index.php/2021/06/19/the-reality-of-caste-discrimination-among-children/

'The first thought that came to mind when I heard about exObjects was to write about the dismantling of my grandparents' home, my summer haven for years. Early childhood memories, and dare I say the most beautiful ones, stem from the nooks and crannies of that home. Come to think of it, from the Madagascar periwinkle flower (sadabahar/evergreen) to the jugnus (fireflies), it feels as if the essentials of our lives were trapped in the rubble, and what remains today is the hope that all of this would be alive again, not merely sit in my memory. The more I dwell on the idea of exObjects, the more I feel it serves as a memory vial, filled with a mix of strange and otherwise unexplored feelings attached to inanimate objects, desiring to be experienced again.'

After a sweltering afternoon, far outside town, we lay on a cot in a mango orchard. Dusk was fast approaching, and despite being called several times to load up our stuff in the cars to leave, all four of us decided to link hands. We lay side by side on the jute cot under the mango tree, staring at the skies. We knew we must wait, and that it would be worth it. We must see the jugnus one last time that year.

Every year it was the same.

As children we thought jugnus were magical because they transported us to unknown realms. Whenever we saw one it stilled the air and breaths of all around. Postures frozen, exchanging whispers of amazement, we chased them through the summer dusk as they guided us out of the shadows of the orchard. In those few suspended moments of being in their company my cousins and I felt invincible, as if there was nothing we couldn't accomplish in the world.

After the scorching sun had decided to rest, the jute cots would be spread out under the guava tree. Mattresses and crisp sheets were unrolled and we knew it was teatime. Nani's snow pigeons were left to wander for a while, plants were watered, tea was poured in china cups for everyone, but this was not what excited us. Such preparations foretold the delights of cool summer evenings in a courtyard near a small pigeon house Nani had built.

There, we spent countless hours with upturned eyes, eagerly anticipating the magic about to happen. More often than not, our long waits were rewarded with nothing but skitting clouds, so, instead, we bet on which would win the starlit races. Occasionally we saw fleeting glimpses of ethereal glows as the jugnus were drawn by the sweet-scented fruits and flowers in the kitchen garden. And when a power cut brought hours of blackout, this was our chance to believe that the world was filled with mystery and enchantment.

Oftentimes, exhilarated to catch a jugnu in the palm of our hands, we dropped it into a glass jar. Then in the dim light of a few hanging lanterns we marvelled and whispered our theories about where glows come from. We decided that minuscule lightbulbs were fitted inside their bodies, and when the light dimmed every few seconds, their power supply was breaking. One of our most trusted theories was that fireflies ate part of the flickering street lamp near the post office in the adjacent lane. When dinner was served, our hushed and heated discussions were put to a stop, and the jugnus were released with a promise that theorising would continue the next day.

Each year, fewer jugnus illuminated Nani's courtyard. It was as if, by growing up, we were leaching the life out of these creatures, their dwindling numbers a testament to our increasing dominion over the natural world.

Eventually, we learned about the depletion of damp, undisturbed places where the larvae grow for months before hatching and the male beetles fly off in the dark. We discovered inside our science encyclopedias that luciferin and the luciferase enzyme react with oxygen to make our jugnus glow yellow. We were amazed to learn that the wingless females convert nearly all of the energy used into light, and that bioluminescence is a more efficient process than anything humans have yet made. We came to understand that the many sources of dazzling artificial lights installed by humans block warnings of danger as well as chances to communicate with and find a mate. Compelled to move away from city lights, jugnus are met with deadly chemical fertilisers and pesticides that protect our crops but threaten their survival.

The thing about growing up is that, while it gives you much to look forward to, it also silently takes away the smallest bits of your life. I envision late-evening sunrays trickling between the leaves of the guava tree, but fail to recall my last visit before that courtyard was knocked down. I'm concerned about losing already waning memories. Addressing them out loud felt too bare, but a communal existential crisis has made us more humane. This thought brings me back to my grandparents' home where everything felt warm and cosy and we only had to wake up each day and have fun. Looking back, I realise we grew up so fast, but those experiences managed to leave a deep imprint on our minds.

With our bustling metropolitan lives, the jugnus are whispers in traffic jams drowned by careless honks. When I occasionally spot them in the bushes and fields alongside the railway track on my journey home, I'm reminded that not all are wiped out by chemicals or exposure to too much light at the wrong time of day. These are the flickering reminders that beautiful jugnus are not confined to a childhood of wonder and innocence, or my lazy evening memories of the past.

Every time the sky turns a cool shade of pink and mellow yellow, it is my memory that gathers the last of the daylight, that watches my tiny hypnotic creatures light up the world one bulb at a time.

A reminder of the beauty and fragility of our planet as well as a symbol of hope and resilience, fireflies, though unseen, still dance.

9

Easy Chair

Shinie Antony

Shinie Antony has written the novels *Eden Abandoned: The Story of Lilith* (Hachette), *The Girl Who Couldn't Love* (Speaking Tiger) and *Can't* (Speaking Tiger), which has been long-listed for the Crossword Book Awards 2024. She has put together the anthologies *Boo* (Penguin), *Why We Don't Talk* (Rupa), *An Unsuitable Woman* (Rupa), and *Hell Hath No Fury* (Hachette). She is the winner of the Commonwealth Short Story Asia Prize in 2002; founder of Bangalore Literature Festival; director of Bengaluru Poetry Festival.

'I have always been a hoarder. I have "new" shoes, clothes, bags and whatnot from years ago – unused, never worn. After a decent period of time, I throw them out with a heavy heart, but not before offending people close to me by attempting to gift them these. In my mind, they are beautiful things I had once upon a time fallen in love with. I have the usual old letters – from parents, brother, friends, fiancé – and art by niece/daughters, mainly of a disproportionate sun rising over stick figures. In my Bengaluru flat, in the kitchen loft, in a cardboard box, is everything I possess. Once in a while I open it and surround myself with photos, greeting cards, little notes passed in class, old essays with teachers' comments and movie-ticket stubs. It's like counting all my money.'

Fishing Net and Tamil Songs

My father came back to our Delhi home looking very sheepish one Sunday. He said he had been to confession, a very Catholic thing to do, especially for someone who last went to church when he wed. What did you tell the priest? we asked.

'That I did not think there is a god,' he said.

'Why would you do that?' my mother gasped.

'I wanted to hear his side,' he said.

This childlike openness and inclusive curiosity – he loved being challenged on just about everything he believed in – made growing up with him a pleasant rollercoaster. And I must say my brother and mother joined in as best they could despite their fondness for sanity and order. Dad was always being Dad, saying the wrong thing, doing the right thing. And it is only when he left us in 2013 that we discovered how like him he had turned us into.

Sometimes we did not know what to do with all his honesty. He revealed everything to anyone who asked. He had no secrets. Lucky for us we don't rob or kill for a living, because he'd merrily have turned us in. Though he would have visited us in jail and told us in excruciating detail what people were saying about us.

Candour was the cure. A mistake made but owned was a moral act. He made it his strength and a source of alarming confidence, this bluntness directed against self. But for those around him it was a muscle relaxant, a spa for the tongue: we could say what we want without fear of judgement. A safe place to unload our moments of mortification. He made it alright with self-deprecating wit; you know, how the exact thing had happened to him … Nothing was too bad or far gone. Everything was retrievable. Everything possible in the second round. Or third.

All anecdotes about him touch on courage and frankness. His funeral, to me, was an endless and exhausting listening in on tales of pluck – like meeting him in a novel. Who was this man constantly changing lanes in rush-hour traffic? It dawned on me then that this was his essence, what he left behind of him: a practical sense, the sheer will to survive, move on, get past. I used to think my parents' constant cheer a middle-class embarrassment while growing up, but now seeing how prone we are to depressive states of mind, I realise what a miracle it was to be brought up by two people who loved each other to bits and let nothing faze them. All solutions were just a punchline away.

The pacemaker in his heart was an object he carried lightly. Hearing from his doctor that a particular patient who had just been dispatched in an ambulance for pacemaker insertion was very nervous about it, my dad decided to literally follow the man. At the funeral, someone walked up to me and said, 'I met your dad just once, when he came to see me in hospital. I was lying there, anxious about my operation, and he just burst into my room and said, "The pacemaker is a thing of joy! Look at me, it has only made my life better." I was astonished to find out how far he had travelled to tell a stranger this!'

When I went through any personal turmoil, there was always his certainty that I'm a fairy tale. I once arrived in Kochi without my suitcase, which got lost at the airport. My saris and jewellery were in it – what would I wear to my brother's engagement, which was the very next day? Before I could even begin to convey my panic, my father said in the most upbeat voice, 'You lucky girl, you are now rid of all the boring old stuff! Let's go shopping right now and pick up everything brand new.' So infectious was his excitement that when a policeman called to say my luggage had been found I could only manage a flat 'oh'.

The easy chair, on which he'd lie to read the newspaper, have his morning tea and generally pontificate on the upcoming day, is with me now. Made of teak, it belonged to his father, and it was with a territorial air that Dad inhabited it. He unfailingly woke up by five a.m. and once the paper came flying over the gate, he hurried with it to the easy chair. Often, we have found him napping under the papers, as if dreaming of all the news he had just read.

I wonder what happened to that fishing net he splurged on when he retired. I belong to a generation that never saw their parents spend on luxuries, so it had been greatly disturbing to hear him go on and on about purchasing a fishing net that we knew he would never use and then have to watch him actually go out to buy it. He spread it out in the hall, though it was too large to be completely unfolded. It covered the furniture and floor, the tiny holes gaping across our daily space, its unused newness in our nostrils. Now and then he would bring the net out of the packing case and contemplate its breadth and length. If we happened to pass by, he would pick up an end and try to show us with gestures how it was to be thrown into the sea. We grew used to seeing him occasionally take this fishing net from the cupboard and smile as if meeting its eye. As a boy he used to go fishing armed with a rod and a worm or two. All his school holidays were spent swimming and fishing in Velur, a village in Kerala, with his maternal grandparents, where he had uncles his own age.

He stood there holding the net, his fingers enmeshed in the nylon of it, his mind back in boyhood. We were careful not to make small talk with him at this point, as that would only bring us to yet another flashback from his schooldays. My mother, who is the quiet type, was the only one who seemed to patiently hear him out, but we always suspected that was because she wasn't really listening.

Watching him wind the clock his father bought in Ceylon for fifteen rupees so many years ago, a clock with a pendulum and a massive black key, was a childhood ritual. We have modernised the clock a bit of late – mother found it hard to wind manually – but the dark warmth of the wood still functions like a vital organ of the wall.

He was also a spectacularly bad singer. It was never the music that glued him to his radio in the first place, but the lyrics. Though he loved old English, Malayalam and Hindi songs, it was Tamil poetry and Tamil lyrics that were his favourite. A lullaby picturised on Sivaji Ganesan, *Malarnthum malaratha* (Like a flower that's started to bloom). A funeral hymn in Malayalam, composed by a German priest, *Samayamam rathathil njan* (In the chariot of time, I tour heaven).

After his abrupt departure – made more abrupt by how talkative a person he had been – these two songs play on a loop in my mind. I can see him clearly as he was then, his head bent a little, eyes closed, palm gently slapping a knee in tune, lips miming the lyrics. Immersed in the alliteration, wordplay, imagery, rhyme … And how he slips into that exact moment he heard it the very first time. I remember the luminous wait on his face in the pause between two words in the middle of a song.

Bangles and Creams

When Mother went through a complicated six-hour hysterectomy or Dad had a pacemaker fitted, neither child was notified or asked for help. After a wildcat bit her, sure she was going to get rabies, my mom just shut the house and waited to die. When she didn't, she got back to work.

The love between my parents was no-nonsense; I always thought she slept in his room because we were one

seventy-nine-year-old ex-military man we knew. *Five?* We stared at him blankly, sure we could reach him if only we knew how.

The man who showed us the same movie twice so we could study the extras or a minor character. Had a barber come home first Sunday every month to give us a crew-cut. Long hair, jewellery, talcum, kohl, posh clothes – he had declared war on these. As a family, we were vain about not being vain.

Then he came off the ventilator. Dad was demoted to dead and there was not a thing we could do about it.

A funeral manager whisked him off for a shave and a bath. The hour we waited for Dad to be spruced up, we were back at the canteen for tea, thinking about what a doctor had just said. That the day he was brought in, Dad had pleaded not to be hooked on to anything that would prolong his life artificially. And we had done just this.

I travelled with Dad in the ambulance. We both maintained silence, a deeply offended one on my part. I was thinking about my funeral phobia; I had managed to evade every funeral until then. My best friend at the age of five, three grandparents, an aunt and sundry acquaintances and neighbours; none had me condoling live at the burial. So this would be my first funeral.

The mobile mortuary kept Dad fresh in our drawing room, ready to greet guests. Nuns placed roses on him. Since the funeral was next noon, the whole night was spent praying by his side. The front door was ajar (it can be locked only after the funeral) and no tea was made at home. Neighbours pitched in seamlessly, used to the rhythm of departures. I could see what Dad meant when he had once said why he wouldn't move out of Kochi to live with me in another city or my brother in a foreign country: 'I am too old to set up home elsewhere and begin this lovely circle of friendships again. It takes a lifetime.'

From the moment he froze on his chair that fateful morning to the last splash of earth on his coffin, there was no dearth of those who wanted to be there for him.

After the seventh-day service in the church, we slept as if drugged. And woke to the implacable hard fact of his disappearance. We can't see his death as anything less than wilful desertion. All his shirts are hanging in his cupboard. His cologne still hits our nose when we open the bathroom cabinet. His toothbrush, his glasses, the book he was reading, his medicines, everything is exactly where he left it. His framed pictures are all over our home courtesy kind relatives, his stamp-size photo is in a newspaper with his birthdate and death date under it.

I know how life works. I understand why a man almost eighty can drop dead. But I also need to know how is he, where is he. I want to tell him everything about the funeral: who came and what they said about him.

Watches and Séances

Our lane, city, state, country, planet is a jumbled address in the middle of nowhere. Do we know the way in? Do we know the way out? We can reclaim our land only with language. When everything is a blur, when all we can see is the mist on our windowpane, what grows is a prescient knowing.

We are but bridges made up of our ancestors' DNA, carrying our fathers and mothers in our cells. We have no choice whom we are born to, but goodness what luck, what magic, to happen by because two people set aside everything else that demanded their attention just to make us, tenderly.

For his last birthday I had given my dad what he called a fancy watch. I don't think he ever wore it. When the hospital returned his things, they also returned his watch; through the fog of grief, I did notice it was the old steel watch, not the one I had given him. For a long time, we held on to both watches, the new and the old. Eventually, his best friend took one and my younger daughter took the other. She got a pretty box and put the old steel watch carefully into it. The box is on a desk in her room in another city.

Once when I snapped that I had half a mind to go to a psychic medium to contact Dad, the same daughter said better not. 'Appappa so firmly believed there's no life after death that if you do manage to track him down, he'd be very embarrassed he got it wrong.'

10

A Tale Of Two Kurtas

Gajra Kottary

Gajra Kottary is a writer for Indian television, with cult and award-winning shows like *Astitva: Ek Prem Kahani*, *Balika Vadhu*, and most recently, *Na Umra Ki Seema Ho*, among others, which have run for thousands of episodes. She is also a novelist and short-story writer. Her published works include the novels *Broken Melodies*, *Once Upon a Star* and *Girls Don't Cry*, and a volume of collected short fiction, *Autumn Blossoms*.

'In the immediate aftermath of the passing of an elderly family member, it's grief that is the most difficult to deal with. The anguish of loss is apparent, but what's not immediately obvious even to oneself is the grief of the unresolved parts of one's relationship with the deceased. And this pain does not go away easily. If anything, it grows with time. Especially when it's the loss of a parent, what nags over the years are the many "what-ifs". Therefore, the belongings of the deceased are a reminder of our own failures to resolve differences in time. My father's kurtas, for example. So, when I set out to write this piece, I only wanted to recollect how, in the process of giving away even the last of his dear belongings, I was letting go. Letting go of my grief for the sake of my sanity. And that, like him, I had finally learnt to not hoard but to give away what was no longer needed. So I could feel a bit more like his daughter than I had done. But in the entire process of writing and reliving my father's peculiar habit of dyeing his kurtas in tea water, I discovered much more about him than that sole idiosyncrasy. A habit that irritated me as a youngster now made me appreciate much more in him that I hadn't understood earlier – his thrift, his creativity in day-to-day life and his sense of childlike adventure. Most of all, his hope even when helpless. Maybe I have finally grown up enough to accept that non-resolution is also resolution.'

What can you possibly write about a kurta?

That the kurta was pristine, that it was sometimes tea-soaked, and the last time it even had bloodstains?

The tale begins with my father's lifelong affair with buying twin kurtas. My father, Pandit Amarnath, was a guru of Indian classical music and the foremost exponent of the Indore gharana founded by his guru, Ustad Amir Khan. He taught music at one of the premier music schools in Delhi, blending the best of the guru-shishya parampara that he so believed in and followed, with some concession to modern needs of convenience and democracy in the teaching of music.

For the last two decades of his life, Pandit-ji was always in a kurta pyjama, both at work and at home. I grew up always seeing him in a kurta. This type of attire admirably suited his profession. Indeed, he looked very dignified in it, with his salt-and-pepper hair, a few strands curling on his forehead completing the look. But I had proof that he had not always dressed so. In photographs of his days in Bombay in the 1960s, where he went to score music for films, he was immaculately dressed in a bush shirt and trousers. Why, oh why, did he have to permanently forsake his shirts for kurtas in my most impressionable years … that was my eternal grouse when I saw the other smartly dressed men around us. But then, I had been born to him when he had crossed forty, considered a bit late for fatherhood.

That grouse would become a sore point for me at the school's annual parents' day function. Thanks to my mother's insistence, I got admitted to a sought-after school, the Convent of Jesus and Mary, New Delhi. There, the duality of my existence was brought out sharply. At home, the ambience was very traditional with classical music thrown in. In school, it was an anglicised way of life.

The standard dress code for fathers at school functions was Western wear. My father, however, would turn up in a silk kurta with an air of insouciance at such events, making me cringe at his desi look. To his credit, I must admit that he carried himself with extreme confidence. Though back then I did a thousand mental somersaults presuming that I would be judged by my friends, their parents and my teachers because of how 'badly' he was dressed. It took me many years to appreciate my father's stand; much later, I respected him for not following the herd. But in those early years, his 'individuality' did give me grief on many occasions.

Looking back, I can say that my father was a perfectionist and a minimalist. Especially when it came to his kurtas. He was meticulous in choosing a particular shade of colour, excited whenever he got his exact shades of beige and off-white silk kurtas at the traditional October sale at Khadi Bhandar. 'There is no point in splurging money by walking into shops whenever one has a desire to buy anything. You can buy the same at a much-reduced price during the festive season,' he would say. His logic could not be faulted. Then once, he did not get either of the exact shades of beige at his preferred sale, and so he settled for a pair of whites. It was then that the experimentation began.

I came home from school one day and found his two new kurtas soaked in different buckets of tea decoction of varying strengths. My cries of surprise, and dare I say disgust, were stifled by my father's explanation that he was trying to infuse the right shade of beige into his kurtas from the tea. Stunned, I blurted out, 'But, Papa, your kurtas will smell of tea!' He chuckled and said they would not.

After hours of soaking and then drying them in the sun, my father stood back to examine his handiwork. He was not exactly pleased, as the resultant shades were not dark enough. And so began another round of boiling tea leaves, soaking and drying the kurtas till the results appealed to my father's sense of colour. As for myself, I was pleasantly surprised to learn that fabrics could be dyed at home!

There was another very singular and emulatory aspect to my father's collection of kurtas: he never shopped indiscriminately. He would only buy a kurta when he sensed that an old one from his collection was beginning to fray. And whenever he purchased one, he would donate the old kurta to a needy person. In that mode of marginal existence, my father's kurta collection never exceeded six: four cotton ones for home wear and two silk ones for formal occasions. He would wear these pastel shades of silk, with dark sleeveless woollen or khaki jackets over them, for his TV recordings or major concerts.

Years later, whenever I felt like going on a shopping spree after malls first came to Bombay, I would remember my father's collection of six kurtas and an invisible hand would tug at me to stop.

I came to Bombay, the city by the sea, after marriage. For someone who wanted to join a creative profession, it was a haven of opportunities and dreams. Much as I wanted my father to visit and stay with me in my marital home, his Punjabi orthodoxy prevented him from partaking of his married daughter's hospitality. Thank heavens my mother felt no such constraints, and stayed with us in Bombay quite often, especially when Delhi went through severe winters.

Sadly, the only time he did come to stay with me was when he was diagnosed with throat cancer and he had to get an opinion at Tata Memorial Hospital. Given his frugality and the seriousness of the visit, I was surprised that he came to the city with his two silk kurtas. For he had decided to dress up to meet my in-laws!

He had to undergo an unplanned minor procedure, which ended up bloodying his kurta. Back home, he was quite anguished to see me, his doting daughter and 'little one', hand-wash the stained silk kurta with mild detergents. But the bloodstains proved stubborn. I kept the kurta aside to have another go at it later.

That very evening, my father suddenly decided to return to Delhi. I was a bit cross as I had expected him to stay with me for a longer spell. He did not say why, and neither did I ask, as I was dealing with a patient who was in pain and who was a senior citizen. I later learnt that he was keen on leaving Bombay as he did not want any invasive treatment, and wanted to depart from this world sooner rather than later, as he had foreseen that he would not be able to sing like before. On the way to the airport, I told him that I would get the bloodstained kurta dry-cleaned and bring it with me to Delhi when I went to look him up.

That was not to be. Weeks later, I heard that my father was critical. As I rushed to Delhi, I wondered if I should pack his kurta and return it to him. But I felt that was not the right time. My father never recovered. Cancer claimed another victim. As I returned to his bedroom after the rites, a wild thought crept in. I went to his sparse wardrobe and picked up the companion silk kurta to bring it with me to Bombay.

The bloodstained kurta and its companion were with me for many years. The use of strong detergents had bleached the stain in the sullied one, and had made the garment patchy; it could not be worn with élan anymore. I had wrapped both kurtas in muslin with a lot of sentiment. Every time I saw the muslin package, I was reminded of the pain my father had suffered when he last wore the kurta. A few months later, I visited a faith healer and she advised me to discard the kurta which had been bloodied. 'This kurta is a symbol of suffering, you must give it away,' she said. Her advice made sense, so I followed it.

The clean kurta I kept for a long time. Gazing at it triggered happy memories: waking up to the sound of him singing every morning, of him recording in the studios of Doordarshan, of him surrounded by a gaggle of his students … I would even laugh as I forgave him his sartorial trespasses at the annual parents' day meets!

Then, one day, his 'little one' finally grew up. I decided to follow his minimalist ways. With a lot of emotion, I gave his kurta away to Shanti Avedna Sadan, the hospice in Bombay for cancer patients. I knew it would bring a smile to my father, wherever he was.

11

Quartet Turned Trilogy

A.T. Boyle

Alison Boyle started out as a copywriter on an international book club magazine in London, a city she had visited once, where she knew no one. She moved to the West County to create books and audio, seeing her first books published in her twenties. Following editorship of a weekly BBC children's magazine she worked as a publisher in Oxford, Cambridge and London. Her writing has been published by Hachette, Penguin, Scholastic, Walker Books and the Turkish imprint Milet. She managed digital awards for the UK government before expanding her arts-based work further north.

Her first story for adult readers was shortlisted for an international award. Set in Istanbul, it was published under the name A.T. Boyle and launched with a dual-language multimedia dramatisation. Following the death of her parents at the height of Covid, their obituaries published in *The Guardian*, Alison began the web magazine *exObjects* at www.artificialsilk.org to explore the imaginative and hopeful aspects of loss. In 2023 she ran the Sadabahar (evergreen) project connecting England with India through story, community outreach and digital.

Chocolate, walnut and pecan cake, Page 171 [A.T. Boyle]

Icing sugar dove, Page 186 [A.T. Boyle]

Night out at the social club, Page 190 [A.T. Boyle]

Gleaming laboratory corner, Page 194 [A.T. Boyle]

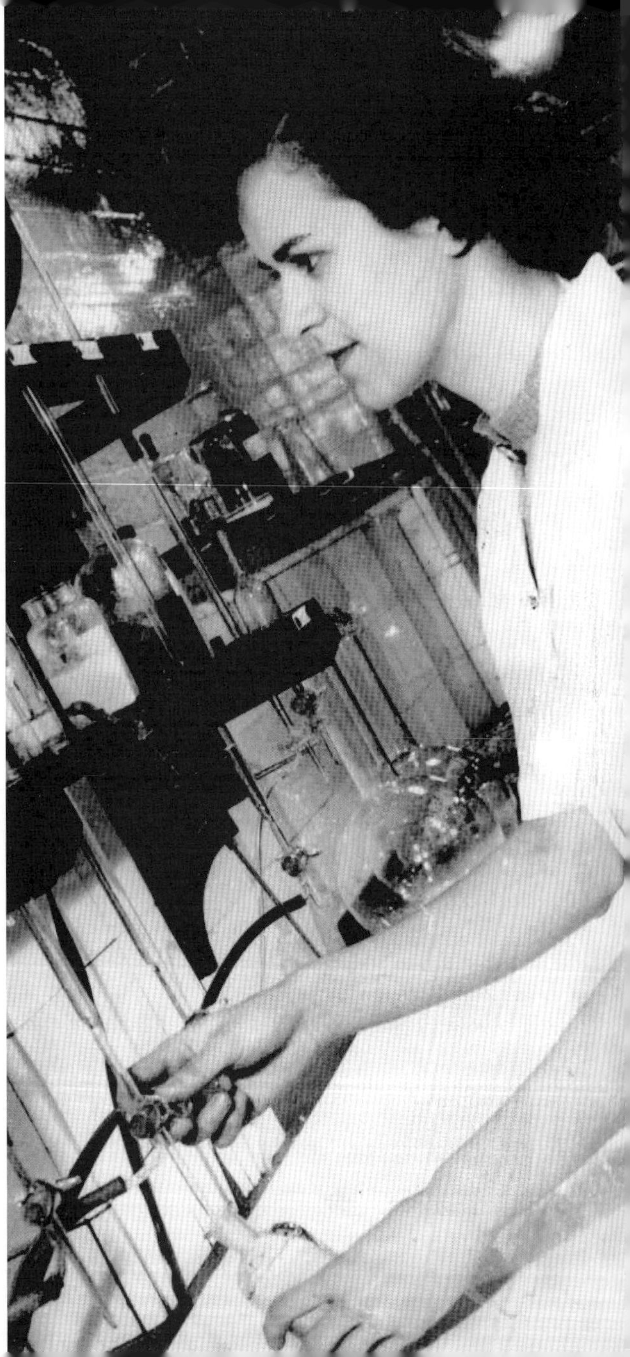

Cameo dress brooch, Page 194 [A.T. Boyle]

A dad acting on stage, Page 201 [A.T. Boyle]

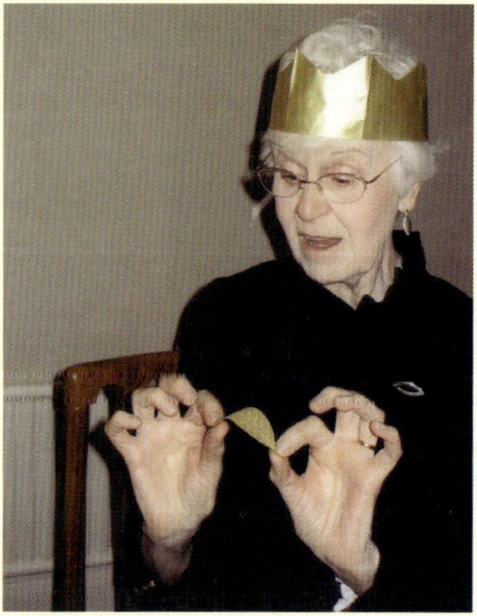

A mum storytelling, Page 201 [A.T. Boyle]

Rose gold watch, Page 203 [A.T. Boyle]

Blue gemstone ring, Page 207 [A.T. Boyle]

'When I was ten, something devastating happened: we missed school parents' night. For a family that ran to the precision tuning of the quiet matriarch who was my mum, this error sent shockwaves through a home where lies were off the menu. Although obviously the children did it, my parents didn't. So, how to respond to someone in authority without fibbing? Dad the wordsmith was out working a factory shift and Mum was so fazed by her household management lapse, coupled with an imperative to tell the truth, that she could think of nothing to write. We sat with scrap pad and pen, poised at the darkening table. The cliché "Due to circumstances beyond our control" appeared in my young mind. I could see my mum thinking that if she wrote these expansive words she wouldn't really be lying, because she had much to juggle, what with her already large family and a new baby and teacher training under way. I carried the note to school next morning. Of course, there were no ramifications; the teachers had heard it before. When I returned decades later to launch a book, the retired headmaster noted his admiration for the way my mum managed her family. I believed him: he'd been responsible for a larger one. The incident rendered visible adult vulnerabilities, and as a child it made me feel relatively grown-up. For this book I have selected some words and objects to create a conceit, so that a few characters who are important to me may persist a little longer.'

It's wonderful to whirl round our sunny garden snipping flowers for a posy. We will be late, reliable in that. I'm taking care not to select what I've grown from the cuttings you gave us. I can't remember them all, thickly interspersed, matching your generosity. It won't matter, though you will notice the mirroring.

About to leave the house when we remember that we forgot your tip of wetting cotton wool to keep flowers fresh in transit. Oh, and the balloons your flautist granddaughter inflated earlier with easy puffs. More minutes late.

Car boot laden with destined-for-the-freezer meals and fruity crumbles and song lyrics if the mood takes us, the satisfactory dong of doors banged shut, seatbelts clipped, and we're off. We sigh self-indulgently, like we've done a day's work. Efforts to support your elderly independence will never balance a lifetime of efforts made on our behalf.

I anticipate taking the sharp corners too fast, so I pester your granddaughter to hold the cake tighter. We've followed your favourite recipe knowing we will never attain the ice-rink smoothness of cakes made for us. So whatever graces are manifested in the object sliding inside a Wizard of Oz tin must be preserved.

The road is pretty clear and soon, but not soon enough, we creep down your driveway in optimal purring mode for a car so ancient. When I apply the handbrake with sensitivity, your granddaughter and I are thrilled to see that our arrival has gone unnoticed. We make ourselves small behind the dashboard and snigger as you re-boil the kettle for the umpteenth time. Are we cruel?

But still we don't move. Instead, we guess what biscuits you've bought to ring the changes, that new-found independence of shopping online. We're bringing gifts, so there will be something for us.

We hope to make you jump at the sound of your own doorbell. We decide that the sleekest move is to only carry the flowers. Arms laden with love, we peer through your kitchen window at close range.

You do jump. We see you hurry to the door in anticipation. Inside we will take turns to hug, to catch the scent in each other's skin, acclimatise to being together after such a long time.

That last part never happened.

You. Us. What next?

Laughter, your granddaughter and I distracted by all the things we need to attend to that are over and above the requirements for party planners.

'It's you who's supposed to be blowing out your candles, Mum! … Shall I blow for you?'

Yes, you nod, instantly happy. Yes.

No pressure on me then. Our family rule is that all flames must be gone in a continuous breath. I mustn't let you down.

I don't want to be the one extinguishing your candles.

Wax flowing over chocolate topping.

Get on with it! I sense you thinking.

The final flame turns restless beacon, then goes out too. All out in one.

We elide the usual questions about how big a slice everyone fancies, and your granddaughter cuts four matching portions for the plates we've brought by car.

And only now is it time for you to stand up and move to the end of the kitchen in slow-motion mime, away from us, not closer. Dad's smiling, going along with the mystery and theatre of it.

Cake slices and flowers and food parcels are posted through as narrow a door slit as can be managed (breathing in before the handle was turned, holding our breaths until the barrier comes down again).

You collect your designated plates in a prison canteen and return to your twin islands.

After the cake has received a quick aesthetic once-over, you take a bite. I think you are pleasantly surprised.

Rewinding the account by half an hour…

We have a good time spying you from the car as you set out two chairs in the precise centre of the kitchen. This furniture is strayed landmass snapped from familiar under-the-table slots.

We struggle to carry everything from the car. There are three doors to enter by. The back where we are headed leads to a small conservatory, its internal door and large glass window opening on to the kitchen where you and Dad are waiting.

You made sure to unlock the back door. We bundle in, late. Freezer meals, sweet and savoury crumbles, flowers protected with a wad of cotton wool inside an elasticated bag, birthday presents chosen for cheer and not utility, everything topples to the floor as we are toppling. Your granddaughter valiantly holds on to her tin. I see that her cheeks are blushed, so she probably nearly dropped it.

We peer ahead at our obedient pupils. We are four actors in an alarming theatrical set.

Our minds whirl with the unquantifiable danger we present to one another. Tentative smiles. The new order offends our instincts to come close. This is not to our habit.

Stalled, two sitting in an overheated kitchen, two standing in a freezing extension, none of us can look beyond the unshatterable glass.

The air shifts, causing our multi-coloured balloons to bob into view, reminding us of your birthday. We silently, individually, ask what we can salvage.

Your eyes anticipate joy. Make of it what we can.

Gestures penetrate the high spec window. Nods, head shakes, words that need repeating. It will be all right, your face tells me. We're doing what we must do.

What your granddaughter and I must do is dip out of sight and crouch behind a cupboard. We must find the candles in the mess strewn across the floor. We must transfer a homemade cake from a tin to a plate without cracking its sponge. We never managed to get the chocolate topping to set, so at least that won't crack.

We must light the candles that spell eighty-nine. Our matches are pathetic. You will have better ones but we can't raid your stores. A few wicks that glowed instantly are chargrilling your imperfect cake.

I peep above the cupboard to see what you are doing. Sitting patiently, wondering why it's taking so long. But you are alert, expectant. Best entertainment in weeks.

At last, your doorstep jesters spring into view and launch a birthday duet of sufficient volume to transcend the double-glazing and hearing loss and physical gulf. We see your mouth move and understand that your small voice is joining in. As the final 'youuuuu' approaches, Dad enters the song too, his full-throated velvet elevating our now purposeful harmonies.

It was good to see you. It really was.

Children during the Second World War, two frail people are tenaciously holding on to self-sufficiency while people who know better are carrying suitcases of embarrassment to events attended by perfect lookalikes. Strict Covid isolation for some, but we saw it in the papers – news at the time and legal findings later.

This awareness of parallel Partygate lives carries the potential for changing course.

Would our family's hands have gripped the shutters we resiled from but willingly pulled down between us? My parents ran to their own code, were responsible to each other and to others. So the answer is probably yes.

Though there were no rules to break, in the end we had to Zoom it.

Hand-made card and presents had arrived by post in good time.

On this occasion everyone has the capability to live-connect and shrink geographic space. Even so, how best to hold a cake and capture it in and out of a room? What would my film-maker father-in-law do?

The cake this year is a sea mine spiked with Hertz horns. Fully ignited, sparks spurt dangerously not only from the top but its spherical sides too. Daughter aims her tech at our computer screen, recording what she can of events unfolding afar. With birthday singing on a loop I'm handed the flaming object, a manoeuvre that requires fresh photographic moves. Now that my hands are full, my partner's are empty. He takes up a gadget so that we can be in this room and the other at once.

Candles are blown in a continuous breath. Once expired, the exploded mine is reduced to something we can begin to eat. I automatically cut three slices and plonk them on the plates.

Pause. Laughter a hundred miles apart. How can our daughter eat her slice? Must she look on indulgently, miffed, studiously translating our comments about sweet airborne wafts and texture on taste buds so that she can elicit a flavour on hers?

Our gap is filled by the conundrum of when four people managed the transference of slices of chocolate cake from one hermetically sealed space to another, a time when we had no choice.

In the present, one slice will pass between the two worlds three people inhabit, echoing the division of four into two in a Lancashire home. Them, us, we, you, all yearning to extend ourselves in close quarter, to savour the scent of ingredients seeping from another person's plate as we eat, not just our own.

This birthday there's nothing for it but to grab my slice and swallow the distance. With every camera now on me, close-ups, probably not flattering, I decide to avoid looking later. Then we forget to be busy with the tech. We become alert to everything that can be absorbed in the moment.

There and here are connected in time and place because we willed it, as we did, not so many years ago.

*

Peace

Trapped in a plastic bag inside a cheap wardrobe is a dove, its delicately pointed wings permanently extended in flight. The focus of many eyes on your wedding cake, this dove must now be considered alongside every other thing you no longer need. Being so tiny, surely there's room to keep a bird that doesn't need feeding?

As though concerned I will not make the right choice, and since you understand the object better than me, it's an unexpected joy to realise we will consider it together.

I was watching your fingers delve to the back of the wardrobe, searching for something practical, an extra blanket, a pillowcase for your growing family? In truth, you were seeking what you rarely allowed: indulgence. Surrounded by bare coat hangers and half-filled rubbish sacks, you notice how much your legs ache. You slump next to me on a bed you no longer need, shoving up closer until we're almost able to touch.

The sheen of the bag forces us to peer through un-dusted glass at our tiny taxidermied specimen. You're puzzled about why you allowed this object to be relegated to the margins. Rather than facing the emotions that begin to rise, your second impulse – which follows quickly – is to run downstairs empty-handed, finish off the housework. The list of chores will always be a list, so I urge us not to ignore our first impulses. Thankfully, this time, we listen.

Loosening the wire round the neck of the bag sets us on a different course from mother, carer, daughter. Like the best of companions meeting for mid-morning coffee, with a tremor of excitement we perch the naked dove on the eiderdown between us, ready to share in something new. I may even get to hear one of your secrets.

We sit at once present and absent looking at the footless bird. Designed to be stuck into a bright white rink of Royal icing, it rolls in my direction. The ancient bedspread breaks its fall and a January sunspot helps us admire the skill required to form a needlepoint beak from sugar and water. Unlike the many statues you and Dad will come across on holiday (emperors' arms, legs, penises, all lost) this beak remains firmly bonded. The bird is neither in flight nor installed on top of a cake. It seems forlorn, separated from its familiars: the baker's Lancashire kitchen, clever sculpting fingers, wedding feast, dark retreat inside a wardrobe. Rediscovered like a found pebble, we cradle the dove in overlapping palms, shocked by the spread of cold across our skin, trying to remember why we kept it.

I hear your muscles click, though the bedsprings don't shift as you stand and move towards the door. You're leaving me to it. I leap towards you in refusal, but your warmth easily contests the case I would have made for you to stay. Half out of the door and still I haven't asked, not directly, if you always hid what you feared the most, requiring the rest of us to read between the lines. Or whether a single catastrophe caused you to adopt the customary mantle. I'll admit I could have been wiser to your finely-tuned manoeuvres, but you would only have become more versatile putting me off the scent. On this darkening afternoon I understand that being the peacemaker entailed subsuming your own needs and desires. More or less happy with this role, even you, an honest woman, surely you stopped to consider how much you could feel at peace when emotions are afforded such fleeting attention.

The door has been left ajar and I'm left to make a decision about the bird. Over the years I witnessed your infuriating disposal of every object you didn't need in a house of seven people and no room for sentimentality. Yet today I discover a loose cake decoration whose value I'm guessing was weighed and re-weighed, and you drew the same conclusion.

I hadn't realised how long it would take to decide which skirts or tops or coats to keep, which of the vast array of shoe lasts with buttons Bluetacked in positions that coincided with your bunions will most remind me of your practical nature and attention to detail. I wish you had kept the wedding dress that you made. I knew which scarves you liked best – the ones you wore on our visits, or was that just another act of diplomacy? When I notice the sharp corners of unused cream boxes and unwanted belts breaking the skin of my rubbish sacks, I panic, thinking I'll have to go through everything again. Your padding across the landing brings some comfort.

Before I entered the room your legacy appeared intangible. But I can see that spending time with you this way helps with definition. A cake was never needed for lift-off. Your footless sugar and water bird was not designed to fly.

*

Possibility

Your family albums are piled against a wall, unsure of their place in lives that run on. I've leafed through the second oldest album in some detail now. Three photos without dates caught my eye.

In one you sit close to a stranger, evening out, white gossamer gloves and Fifties cream dress (probably homemade) lending an air of elegance to the social club setting. Arm in arm with your fiancé Roy, his dark suit and upright bowtie complement the care you've invested. Both aged about twenty, with equal warmth you meet the requirements of an unnamed photographer. Neither subject yet wears an engagement ring.

On the same page is a photo of Roy in studio pose, this time seated alone and carefully cross-legged. Everyone from that period looks older, so I'm guessing it's a twenty-first birthday projection of his future life. Confidence and promise shine through. Roy has selected subtle-striped tweed and a racy spotted tie that's knotted to perfection. I like the look of Roy. Dad and you always agreed he was a lovely man, important but bland information about someone you intended to marry.

The equanimity you mastered in the seventy years following Roy's death, which at times kept your large family afloat, gave no hint of suppressed secrets relating to this man, so a stranger might admonish me fairly for not interrogating you while I had chance. But I know there was slim chance of revelation. You held onto privacy like a bundle of fresh eggs. Laid by an aunty's hens out of town, you nestled the secrets in your lap, ferried them weekly by bus, colluded early in your mother's subversion of postwar rationing, a child less likely to be suspected.

I must accept that I will never hear anything specific about Roy's kindness, his wit, what he loved most about you, how you learned of his death, who you turned to when he was gone.

What follows immediately from the two Roy photos in the same album is smiling representations of you (with parents and siblings against a manicured council house garden, family grouping on a sandy beach). I can't understand how such images can be congruent because you appear perfectly happy.

I turn the page and you're out on a date with Dad. Ring fingers are out of shot. How many months passed between having Roy on your right and Dad sitting in his place? Given the expense of photography, what am I to understand about the timeframe of your determination to move on? I'm imagining that you and Roy each acquired a print of your night out, the beginning of something important, and unless he was vain or you asked him, perhaps the studio pose was donated by his family, a graveside act of condolence, a sharing of grief? Two renderings of someone you were planning to spend the rest of your life with isn't much.

When I place my three images side-by-side (as you did not intend them to be) Roy's complexion appears paler than Dad's, which began Irish pale and turned at most ripe raspberry after dedicated hours of tanning. Roy's lips and hands appear podgier. I like the way Dad's long fingers intertwine yours. I like knowing that his wayward tie and open smile, a lit cigarette poised confidently between the fingers of his other hand, said nothing about his faithfulness. (Returning from a work conference, I remember his outrage at seeing married colleagues fall into bed so easily with others.)

Your blackbird eyes look out at me, electrified, daring me to enjoy your new beginnings, to experience your hopes. I remember these eyes in later years as more demerara than muscovado, by then wearied by motherhood or breadwinning or an unhealthy obsession with housework. Dad's thick hair is Brylcreemed dramatically, and a perm undulates the ramrod locks you were born with. But Roy's hair appears to flow as naturally as the ship doodle I later heard he had made for your brother, you taking time to come down for the date. Sailing was never a subject of family conversation, suggesting aspirations beyond the tight-knit Northern community that was your eventual course.

Just when I'm about to leave my tour, a little dissatisfied, I flip Roy's studio portrait. An ink-blue stamp identifies the factory photographer commissioned to take your wedding photos in 1954. I realise that you must have all been colleagues in the textile factory joined as teenagers, that Dad will have seen you and Roy together, and you will have seen Dad with the other 'girls' described in his initial love letter. I would not understand why you chose Roy first, because you did not tell me yourself. The *Roy was a lovely man* duet must have incorporated an acceptance that, if he had not died, Dad would not be wearing the wedding ring you pushed onto his finger.

Efforts to find Roy's grave are not helped by no one knowing his surname, the name you would have taken on marriage.

In the imagery of Roy lies a dual possibility: that you might have lived a more open life where emotions weren't hidden so deep because the man you wanted to marry had not died. And that you may never have had children, never mind five. If Roy had lived, if you had spent your lives together, a certainty is that I would not have grown in your womb, you would have not been my mother. I would not have existed. And, your children would have been spared the fission that occurred at your death, when your clever architecture became quickly overwhelmed.

Fragile, modest strength persists through a far-reaching signal. I must listen hard because your voice has quite gone. Maybe I can accept what you said, that you lived a very happy life, made possible (though you liked to chat) because of your huge capacity to hold and not divulge. And, maybe I must forgive your inscrutability because your reasons were bigger than yourself.

*

It's Chemistry

The 1950 photographic portrait of a woman interacting with chemistry equipment reveals someone I know and a scenario I do not.

Although I heard many stories of the local cloth that replaced cotton – artificial silk – I didn't visit my parents' Lancashire laboratory, so this rare image is my chance, my only chance, to peer in. Aged around twenty, that independent woman is younger than my daughter, although the combination of popular hair-wave and prim and proper nature makes her look older. Surrounded by translucent glass phials in the orderly corner of an artificial silk factory, here is my mum.

White coat sleeves turned stylishly and falling just below the elbow, veined hands I remember from the long years running up to her death now reversed to plump flesh, caught mid-action, the woman in the photograph is fulfilling some kind of process. Her serene mouth is at the upper end of the Mona Lisa spectrum. While my dad talked exuberantly about the same lab, starting a year earlier at fifteen, Mum recalled this particular task – titrations – as b*o*ring, loading the o with disparaging elongation, her dose of reality squishing attempts to romanticise.

The profile view unites with the times she was glimpsed in home mode, commandeering a hoover, kitchen sink, washer, pan on the boil, weekly shop, garden spade. Later, retraining as a schoolteacher, she ran her family with precision alongside. In retirement the minutiae of housework and caring for my dad above her own health were as carefully balanced as the housekeeping books (to the penny).

But this laboratory is no workaday scene, and it was only recently I understood where its fiction lies.

Her factory employer, Courtaulds, needed customers for its miles of durable filaments, an affordable alternative to real silk. Alongside glossy colour brochures and sample kits distributed by sales people, the medium of moving film would be harnessed to create a super-professional tool that cut through in global markets.

I recalled the story of a documentary crew sent in by bosses. Scrubbed-up processes and product would be celebrated, while a model workforce would play supporting roles. No wonder the tiles in my mum's corner gleam, why her curvaceous glass phials are so reflective of light on that auspicious advertising day.

One of several settings selected for the crew's storyboard, this is a key quality-control stage in making artificial silk. Probably elided in the film were the many corrosive alchemical stages that turned the amber honey-like viscose derived from pine trees into miles of threads for weaving clothes and sanitary towels and parachutes and car tyre webbing.

Another woman's profile featured in my mum's limelight that day. A newly seen photograph I inherited reveals a piece of jewellery I half-recognise. There it is, peeping from the top of her lab coat. I had given it little attention. This brooch measures 3 x 3.5 centimetres (I know, because I rushed to find my odds and ends box). I estimate it to be a cheap Roman Diana replica, or a Jane Austen derivative of a cheap Roman Diana. The profile of the ivory-skinned woman is no unique portrait, and has been pasted onto a marble effect shell base. Metal filigree skirting an oval perimeter is tarnished but undamaged. Traditional drapes at a pert bosom are pinned by a flourish of flowers on the deity's shoulder. A four-petalled flower sits above the ear. The hair resembles tail feathers plucked from an exotic bird.

I feel glad it's a reproduction and didn't exploit sea creatures for human enjoyment.

I look at the reverse and notice the horizontal fastening pin. It's a little bent but well-made, with no sign of repair. I'm surprised by the cold feel of the tawny-pink marble, which leads me to think that, after all, it might be original helmet or conch shell. Maybe my cameo is an equal thirteenth to the twelve caesars drowned by 1588 rocks at the Giant's Causeway. My mum's father would never tell his ancestry. He and his emerald-eyed wife with a gemstone ring to match stayed tight-lipped. But the tone of my mum's skin, browning to a deep Spanish Armada the moment sunshine touched it, tells its own story. Irish lass and shipwrecked sailor, went our unsolved legend, sparkling the grind of social status in a post-industrial city.

The brooch my mum wore to work occupies a tiny proportion of the factory photograph, so I let myself off for missing the detail. You see, I am often drawn to her eyes, alert, focused on their task. Or, I find myself scrutinising the exposed arms that first held me. Or, I reach out to touch a hand when I am no longer able to in life.

I bring the cameo closer to its photographic representation and see other pairings of note. I followed my mum to a secondary school run by nuns, the Faithful Companions of Jesus. Whilst her aptitude in chemistry led to a job that made use of her talents, the single-sex education intended to encourage females to excel without male distraction didn't make the sciences any more appealing to me. I recall the drama of being let loose on Bunsen burners, Petri dishes, phials that looked like they would break if breathed on, and well, that's it. There were no questions I answered quickly or correctly, although there is a slim chance I may be doing myself a disservice.

Close in age, my mum and I stood at exactly the same chemistry bench.

That factory morning, heart racing in anticipation, a young woman arranged her carefully permed hair, fingers riffled through a trinket box, something to embellish the neckline of a jumper. Finally alighting on the raised mound of a Diana brooch, she quickly pinned it as she called goodbye to her mum and counted out coins for the bus.

On entering the gates she raced up the back steps two by two, heard the hum of strangers' voices behind worn lab doors, saw lights being assembled on poles, wires everywhere, conjoined wires, a trip hazard, they warned. At her bench the woman was told to clasp a bottle and a switch, to fix the muscles in her long fingers and arms so that the camera crew can catch her mid-experiment. She must hold the natural smile that will be found appealing by buyers worldwide.

A missing object I made efforts to find is the film itself. My dad the showman became increasingly exercised about its loss; it featured him too. Had he told me before the 2,500 workers received redundancy notices, the possibility of finding a company archivist who valued something other than asset stripping would have been higher. He loved his job and saw the film as part of his legacy, a permanent record of him in the world, a lad who started out with the love of two parents and a determination to express himself through work and creative endeavours. I have not come across a photo of him at a chemistry bench, although in other places I have told some of his many stories.

Before I close the factory door, I'll point out a difference you may have noticed. My mum's profile diverges from the pert nose of her refined cameo Diana. I wonder how many people sported that kind of nose in Roman times (the shape I hankered after), and how many bore a Roman nose. Of course refinement can be suggested through the physical features we are born with, but choosing to wear an object that makes us feel refined perhaps enhances the values within. However cheaply bought, this brooch is cared for.

I take with me a discovery. We cannot rely on the fact that an elegant cameo pinned at a fine young neck signifies that jewellery was allowed at work, and I'm convinced my apparently conventional mum occasionally ignored the rules. I did not see her this way until I made time to look.

*

Gold Leaf

I was the changeling who rebelled against convention while growing on its vine. As you know well enough, I rebelled against the neat imperative to comply, what a woman must do. If you had been born when I was born, we might have found the language to chat like the sister I never had. When sitting silently on adjacent chairs, motherly role dispelled, as sympathetic equals we might more often have articulated what shimmered under the surface. We might have seen the emotional awkwardnesses, a common desire for self-protection, as the unnecessary barriers they were.

Under the carapace of conformity you dreamed in colour and shape and pattern. When I dreamed of my new toddler wearing the non-pink dungarees I couldn't find in shops, you tape-measured her legs and body, created the pattern, tie-died the wholesome cotton cloth, machine stitched the seams, hand sewed the buttonholes.

Whenever I offered praise you laughed, indulgent like a mother, but that habitual edge of reality rebuffed me too. A child of the War, you were never too weak for this learnt modesty to kick in. 'You give me too much credit!' said more than once. Sometimes I think I convinced you.

Dad was the out-and-out entertainer. Once he had our attention he could conjure a person, real or imagined, give you the bump of seeing them again. Or for the first time. From the age of fifteen he donned wigs and beauty spots, was the noble lord and the nasty grand inquisitor. He wore silk shirts and cashmere jumpers for publicity shots (and I hope regretted returning them to the wardrobe mistress). He was dramatic in youth clubs and on the grand stages of Victorian church halls. He serenaded people in working men's clubs and care homes, drawing on that knack of making people present in the crease of a mouth, a gesture, a well-judged expression. He was able to be at once intimate and self-deflecting.

He rehearsed for hours, was a natural too. In dapper jacket and neat-pressed trousers, neckerchief held aloft with nifty wire, we lack a soundtrack or video but a two-dimensional image can belt out his exuberant Oklahoma song at equal volume, inciting everyone to rush to the fields and pluck ripened corn.

As we saw, Dad captured what is universal, making patent what is otherwise inexpressible. He became the velvet-voiced storyteller, bedtime hair-brusher, joker, mischievous partner at the other end of a seesaw. Sometimes his fierce need for self-expression in the public sphere – theatre and singing – saw him commit family time on his own terms.

You were different.

When I put you on the spot, atmosphere just right, you held the room, our quiet entertainer. On these rare occasions I inhabited the story that sprang from your fleetingly assured lips, a small leaf of gold paper suspended between your fingers, a prop pulled from a pile I'd assembled for our challenge.

You lived in the shadow of louder warblers. But when I cornered you and you knew there was no escaping, in those spontaneous flights of fancy you were the one who excelled.

*

Watched Over

It was you who caught me wandering corridors when others slept. You who led me back quick enough to enjoy still-warm sheets, saving me from an electric blanket whose current ran through flesh and made fingers vibrate against wallpaper. You who hid my toddler birthmark from attention by buying long cotton socks when the fashion was summer short. You who absorbed my complaints about the heat, who looked unswervingly to me.

You who gave me the rose gold watch given by your husband on your wedding day, or maybe it was your first anniversary. A gift to me at Christmas when I was twenty-two, swapped for a modern design selected by Dad that I didn't like and I'm not sure you did either.

You who didn't complain when that rose, that old gold, was instantly lost. You who helped sift the wrapping paper to no avail. Forgave me it was gone too soon. Embraced me when I returned from the dustbin outside, green sprout-adorned watch found, happiest for my re-found happiness.

When I missed you, working far away because that's where the jobs I wanted to do were, I held your watch up to my ear, its fine Swiss tick like your fast heartbeat, sounding like us together: sometimes nervy, sometimes not able to say, held fast by our foundations.

In the present I don't wear our watch. I'm afraid I'll lose it.

When you died I remembered where it was safely stored. I observed the time it had stopped: just before 10.30 in the morning. There's no significance in that. There's no reason to leave the winder unwound.

Don't over-wind, comes your voice. Always that clear instruction to take due care, the frisson of worry, a How will we manage? And, Get on and wear it!

This is what being watched over feels like: someone alert to you, who wants to worry over you. It irritates, but pleases too. Sometimes beyond words.

*

Soundwaves

Here is a room that sees little sun, so we are not drawn to it. A ghost pile of board games, an empty table big enough to seat a noisy family, a piano silenced by children leaving home to lead divergent lives. Not a modest room exactly, but rarely used.

'It's Mum here' still resonates from the corner of this room, across a longer distance now, and requiring manipulation of the button on an answerphone. Her musical phrase sometimes contains a modifier: 'It's only me.' And while we know it was both of them, that my once-noisy dad was listening by her side, she is only referring to herself.

We hear a hope to catch us in our busy lives, we who adopt answerphone management techniques. Our routines rarely coincide: we have just started eating, are in the middle of a deadline, are not ready with the information we promised to impart by the time of the call, or we are simply not in the mood. We will call back. She knows. Mostly it isn't because we are out that we don't answer, or even that we are busy. She knows this too, and that it's a happier experience for all when stories to pepper their increasingly closed-in days are imparted with gusto.

I was surprised when I played the pitch of her voice on the piano. I already knew that the stress falls in the middle, on 'Mum' and 'only', but the musical sounds brought greater emphasis, something about her efficiency and economy, how she appreciated and was not in competition.

A pair of three words compressed in singsong syllables reminds me of her truth-seeking dead stops, where a failure to react with more than a weak smile told the speaker they had taken the wrong tack. Our flimsy machine is no match for the layers of self-deprecation and deceleration, her practised ability to absorb like a railway buffer.

Now that I am the mediator of her message, the intimate parts are of my choosing, whether to leave in or take out.

An audio sting, heard hundreds of times across my lifetime and thousands of times in hers, reverberates without need of a machine: it is lodged in our ears. I gain comfort from hearing a few words said the way she wanted to say them.

*

Indian Sapphire

Someone mounted a gemstone in a circle of rose gold. The sapphire was blue, step-cut.

India. Exact time and location? The kind of life led by miner and jeweller? Never to be known.

'Do us a favour, pick up a ring for my dad while you're out there. Wedding anniversary coming up.'

'What's their budget?'

'Haven't the faintest. We will top up any shortfall. Nothing over-dear, mind.'

A textile salesman making routine visits to India bought the ring, ticked it off his list, carried it back to England.

Boxed ring handed over in a factory where the salesman and my parents worked. Decent price. How much, will never be known. All other India-side circumstances, will never be known.

Delivered by my dad to the tired, cigarette-stained hands of a foundry worker.

My shy granddad gave the box to his wife. Exactly when, I will never know.

'Oh, Frank!'

An eternity ring.

A sapphire pushed over the chubby knuckle of a Preston cotton weaver.

At the end of their terrace was a high wall, the back wall of a factory where my grandma mastered four looms for forty years. Their community holidayed in Wakes Week, a different slice of summertime allotted to each Northern weaving town or there would be no room in the trains or hotels. A time for the machines to be cleaned, serviced, readied by the handful of neighbours left behind.

The furthest these two people travelled was by boat to Ireland, where the man still had family. The rest of the time it was Pontin's holiday camps, a touch of glamour with heated swimming pool, fish and chip shop, betting shop, bingo hall, ballroom. Their individual pre-fabricated chalet was an immobile version of present-day cruising cabins, and once on-site, a heady sense that everything was free constituted the luxury.

'Oh Annie!' admired her holiday friends. 'Where'd that come from?'

Mostly it was day trips to Blackpool and staying in B&Bs. Sometimes we would go together, eat fish paste sandwiches made with precision by my mum, take a risk with periwinkles on the seafront, hooking out the worms with a dressmaker's pin.

The foundry worker died.

One Sunday dinnertime the ring was taken off the weaver's finger and extended towards her granddaughter.

'Grandma!'

Waves of Catholic guilt. Had the young woman coveted her neighbour's goods? She had always admired the ring, couldn't remember doing it outwardly.

Two bone structures wildly different, yet the ring needed no alteration.

No words to describe the gesture. Circumstances at birth and a denial of education shut down expectations and opened generational gulfs. High windows opaqued by cotton fibres, the mechanical clamour of repeating looms, these things could no longer be fathomed. Homemade gestures passed woman to woman containing news of babies, periods, rows, sickness, finance, jokes. Watchful overseer eyes and a voice that shames my grandma for a few slubs found in cloth, docked wages the least of her hurt. She told me this, I felt her dinted pride.

A legacy greater than four decades of sapphire carried on the marriage finger of a different hand.

A chance to journey wherever the next generation planned to go.

A state of evergreen, *sadabahar*, arising from reinvention and being alert to opportunities in the present.

A reminder of how long ago my connections with India began.

Acknowledgements

Thanks to Shantanu Ray Chaudhuri, whose excitement for publishing this book means we have an object to hold and read, the intangibles contributed by its authors finding a permanence of sorts.